Born A BASTARD Now BORN AGAIN

ELDER ALFRED L. CALVERT

Unless otherwise indicated, all Scripture quotations are taken from the King James Version of the Bible.

Book cover design & page design by
Simpson Communications 248.443.9880
simpsoncommunications@comcast.net

Born A Bastard, Now Born Again
ISBN 978-0-9728560-0-3
Copyright © 2002 by Elder Alfred L. Calvert
16000 W. Nine Mile Road, Suite 422
Southfield, Michigan 48075

Published by Alfred L. Calvert Publishing
16000 W. Nine Mile Road, Suite 422
Southfield, Michigan 48075
To order more copies of this book call 248.424.8424

Printed in the United States by Morris Publishing
3212 East Highway 30
Kearney, NE 68847
1-800-650-7888

Dedication

I dedicate this book from Jesus Christ Who is Lord of all, to everyone who has or is embracing the street life. I dedicate and proclaim that you will be washed by His Word, sprinkled by His Blood, sealed by His Spirit, and saved by His Grace. I dedicate this book to you by the mercies of the only true and living God.

Born A Bastard, Now Born Again

Preface

These four phases of my life are factual in nature, unique in character, a comparison may be made between my life phases and the "potter and the clay" analogy where God deals with man as He sees fit. It also indicates the power of the only true and living God who can take man's life in full circle and bring it back to Himself for His glory.

The pimp is well-groomed at all times. So is the preacher. The pimp possesses persuasive power and talks for his money. So does the preacher. Troubled women come to the pimp for counseling. Likewise is the ministry of the preacher. The pimp directs the soul to the devil. Hopefully, the preacher directs the soul to the Lord. God looks beyond the position of the pimp and sees his potential as a preacher.

The poison intimates the dope dealer who lives well, drives the luxury car, and controls the neighborhood with the power of the dope. The preacher likewise lives well, drives the luxury car, but controls the neighborhood with the power of the Word of God. The dope dealer possesses the false power; the preacher possesses the Holy Spirit, the Real Power. Again, God looks beyond the position of the dope dealer and sees his potential as a leader in the community. The tenacity it takes to live for the devil is the same tenacity it takes to live for the Lord. However, with God, all things are possible.

The prison is a wilderness experience, a proving ground, a boot camp for the pimp/dope dealer, who according to God's foreknowledge, eventually preaches. It is time well spent when God and man commune together. The Bible explains in Hebrews 12:11 that if man practices righteousness during the time of punishment, he will come out with the fruits of peace.

The pimp/dope dealer is stripped of all pride and is found as nothing without God where true repentance begins, and God teaches the man in a classroom directly from Heaven.

The preacher who was once a pimp/dope dealer is now called to preach the Gospel of Jesus Christ in prison where he has to preach against all odds. It is here where God shows His power and assures His preacher that, "No man can stand before him all the days of his life. As I was with Moses, I will be with thee, and no weapon formed against thee shall prosper."

Preaching is the highest office in the land. It is the only office that leads natural life into eternal life. I'm happy to hold that office knowing that, "I Was Born A Bastard, but Now, I'm Born-Again."

Alfred L. Calvert

Acknowledgements

Thanks to the only wise God for His foreknowledge and the tools He used to save my soul: the prosecutor who prosecuted me and the judge who sentenced me long enough for God to save me.

Thanks to Dr. William H. Murphy, Sr., pastor, author, teacher, and founder of the Greater Ebenezer Full Gospel Church. He is a wise man who taught me pastoral ministry for three years. Thanks also to the Greater Ebenezer family for the numerous times they put up with my preaching.

Thanks to Bishop Charles H. Ellis, III, my pastor and the greatest leader of today. Thanks to the Greater Grace Temple family, especially Elder Spencer T. Ellis, my friend and prayer partner.

Thanks to Bishop Noel Jones, the greatest preacher on this planet who gave me the opportunity to minister at Greater Bethany in Los Angeles, California. It was one of the greatest times of my life.

Thanks to Bishop Clarence and Dr. Joyce Hadden who always encouraged me.

Thanks to Bishop Johnny J. Young, pastor, author, scholar of the Church of God Pentecostal in

Inglewood, California who God uses to open doors for me beyond my dreams.

Thanks to Bishop R. Williams and the many pastors who have allowed the Spirit of God to invite me to preach to their congregations.

Thanks to Vernon Isby, CEO of the Gospel Connection Newspaper and Earlene Cooke Edwards who the Lord uses mightily in my life. Thanks to the saints who have spoken life into my ministry.

Thanks to Pam Perry for encouragement and Diane Reeder who helped to edit and soften the language of this book.

Thanks to my best friends George Cameron, Ray Jackson, and Virginia Slappey, the most wonderful woman on planet Earth, and to my two children, Al Jr. and Kim Calvert.

Thanks to Ella Mae who birth me, my aunt Mildred who raised me, the street life that gave me, and to Jesus Christ Who saved me.

Table of Contents

Born A Bastard, Now Born Again

Introduction

Individuals from all walks of life should appreciate this book by Elder Al Calvert. Many of us who are call *"pew babies"* can thank God for sheltering us from the ever-present dangers and dark sides of society. While on the other hand, those who are yet struggling with various substances and a need to impress others with abundant materialism at any cost, can grasp a hope and trust that only God can offer. God has blessed Elder Calvert to share with his readers a glimpse of this earthly "gold-plated" road that most times lead to death and destruction.

Proverbs 16:25 reads, *"There is a way that seemeth right unto a man, but the end thereof are the ways of death."* Elder Al Calvert, through the medium of transparency, has disclosed some of his most personal experiences in this book. As you journey with him, one can only greatly appreciate the grace of God as Al is rescued from the valley of death and is transformed into the kingdom of God. He candidly and with great detail discusses his preoccupations with wealth, lust, and pride. The Scriptures tell us in *I John 2:16, "For all that is in the world, the lust of the flesh, and the lust of the eyes, and the pride of life, is not of the father, but is of the world."* This book brings this biblical truth to life and warns of the deception and lies fostered by Satan.

As you read this book, you will be encouraged by the awesome demonstration of the power of God and its availability to ordinary people who will forsake their ways and look to Jesus, who is the "Author and Finisher of our faith." Allow this writing to bless you. There has to be at least one person with whom you can share this book. Believe me, it will make a profound difference in his or her life.

Bishop Charles H. Ellis, III
Senior Pastor
Greater Grace Temple
Detroit, Michigan

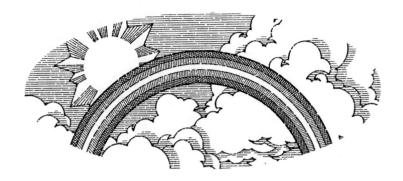

The Birth

November 1, 1945. It's about 7:45 P.M. in Brighton, Alabama, a town so small you could blink and pass through it. A man-child is born. A midwife, Miss Georgia Young, helps him into this world. My grandfather, Solomon Calvert, looked at me and said, " He's such a little *fellow*." So *Fellow* became my nickname.

My name is Alfred Lewis Calvert. I grew up in the family home with my Grandfather, Solomon Calvert, my mother Ella Mae, and her husband Reuben Heard Jr. It meant nothing to me as a child that the man I knew as my daddy was called Mr. Heard, and that my last name was Calvert, because everyone called me Fellow anyway, and the two different names were rarely mentioned together or talked about. I just knew that Mr. Heard was my daddy.

I have come to realize that after my birth, Mr. Heard loved my mother enough to marry her. I believe my grandfather Solomon convinced them to let me carry on the family name of Calvert.

A Good Start

I was Ella Mae's first born; she took me everywhere she went. She was active in the PTA, helping me to adjust to going to school for the first time. I can still remember being crowned king at our "May Day" festival at Brighton Elementary School. My mother used her skills to make my white satin suit which consisted of a white satin bloused shirt, knickerbocker pants, and a red and gold trimmed royal cape. She had to be proud of me as I marched around the school playground with my May Day queen, Jocelyn Boyd. We watched the May Day festivities as we sat on the throne prepared for us. My mother assisted me in my efforts to be king. Her efforts helped to make this day possible. It was one of the proudest moments of our lives together. I never wanted this day to end, not knowing that in a few short years Ella Mae would be gone forever.

Divine Encounter

I must have been five or six years old when my mother took me to a revival and sat me down on the mourners bench. That's where you sit every night until you accept Jesus. I felt so alone until the preacher got my attention. Rev. Norwood preached that famous sermon, "The Eagle Stirs Her Nest." He began to talk about how the mother eagle will throw the young eaglet out of the nest so that it can learn to fly on its own. Everyone had gone up to take the preacher's hand except me. I wanted to go just to get off the bench, feeling somewhat foolish sitting there alone. I began to look around for my mother to receive some type of sign to come to her, but the mother eagle had left the young eaglet to fly on its own. I could not see anyone, for a bright light had blinded me. Then I could see the hand of the preacher extended toward me, and even it looked as if it were a light. I left the mourner's bench weeping to take the hand of the preacher.

Now I know this was my first encounter with the Lord Jesus. The Bible teaches us to bring up a child in the ways of God. I was baptized in the river, and continued to participate in Christmas and Easter programs, and sad to say that's all Jesus was to me–a program. I also thought that He was white with blue eyes.

Parents, it is most important that we teach our children the Word of God daily, line upon line, precept upon precept, here a little, there a little. We must introduce Christ to them at a young age. We must also make Christ attractive to them, even Him hanging on the cross, and convincingly expound upon how He rose from the dead, because that's the power of God unto salvation. I've learned that before I saw the bright light in Shiloh, before I was formed in the womb of Ella Mae, God had already ordained my life.

A Mother's Love

Mr. Heard was a loving, kind man who always showed me the love of a father. He and my grandfather Solomon were the perfect father figures. Shortly after I was born, Mr. Heard married my mother and soon to follow were the births of my brother Ron and my sisters, Carolyn, Shirley, and Martha Faye. When I was eleven and my youngest sister Martha was two years old, our mother, Ella Mae, passed. This was the darkest day of my life.

Our relatives decided that my brother Ron, my middle sister Shirley, and my youngest sister Faye should live with Poppa and Emma Heard, the parents of the man I thought was my daddy. My oldest sister Carolyn went to live with our aunt and uncle, Mr. and Mrs. Clemon Davis. I stayed in the family house with Mr. Heard and my grandfather Solomon. I'm the only child who does not have his last name, but we remained together after our mother's death. No one could make me believe that he was not my father. Even today I believe a father is the one who cares for the son, and not necessarily the one who just had sex with the woman.

It's true that life goes on, but there is no love like a mother's love. Mr. Heard continued to take care of me, working hard in the coal mines during the day and coming home every night to tend to my needs.

He went to work every morning, but always had breakfast with me before he left. In the summer we fished and in the winter we went hunting and brought home rabbits and squirrels to skin and cook. On Sunday you found us in church. Even with the security of his care, I would often get lonely for my mother. Oh, how alone I was, and how confused I was about this God who allowed my mother to die so young, leaving me without a mother's love.

My brothers and sisters, please show love one to another while you have a chance. No matter what the situation, come together as a family unit as often as possible.

Author of Confusion

Now to further compound my fears, loneliness and confusion, Lucifer himself detained me when I was twelve years old, one year after my mother died. Reality had set in and I knew that she would never come back to me. Reality became a sharp dagger that pierced my heart. My constant thought was, "I am going to be alone in this world, a motherless child."

Satan approached me one day coming up the hill from Moses Lipscomb's corner store. I was hurrying home, desperately trying to get to my evening chores, which consisted of bringing in the coal and wood to make fire to heat water for cooking and for taking our baths. These chores had to be done before my daddy, Mr. Heard, came home from work at the

Mulga Coal Mine. This was not God's woman who stopped me in my tracks. I understand now in my saved life that she was a woman sent by Satan to discourage me. He is the enemy of our souls, and he did confuse me. The woman detained me, saying, *"Did you see your daddy Tom Johnson when he was here from Detroit?"* At this point I'm now more confused than ever. I knew nothing of this Tom Johnson; all I knew was the daddy who had taken care of me for as long as I could remember. My twelve-year-old mind, still reeling from the death of my mother, had another reality with which to contend.

I've since learned that God is not the author of confusion, but in His sovereign will for our lives and especially for our salvation, He will allow certain things to happen to us, things that seem bad but turn out to be blessings once we go through them. **In Isaiah 55:8-9, we read, *"God's thoughts are not our thoughts, and our ways are not His ways."*** My confusion was understandable. I had never heard the name Tom Johnson. All I knew was that my daddy was Reuben Heard. The truth that I was born out of wedlock, fathered by a man I had never seen, came before I was ready for it.

> "When I heard that I was a bastard child, my mind started spinning out of control. What did that mean?"

Through idle conversation I once heard someone say that any child born out of wedlock was a bastard child. When I heard that I was a bastard child, my mind started spinning out of control. What did that mean? Was I less of a person because of my status? I was hurt and confused, a motherless child, realizing that the man I loved as my dad was not my dad, and that a child born out of wedlock was and is a bastard. Although I didn't know the full meaning at the time, I knew it did not sound good. That word "bastard" hurt me all of my life, and nobody knew it but God and me.

Just trust Him. He can bring you out of anything. When things seem out of control, please remember God is in control. Read the story of Joseph in the book of Genesis, beginning with chapter 37. If Joseph's brothers had not thrown him into a pit because of his dreams, he would have not been sold as a slave into Egypt. Had he not gone to Egypt, he would have never met Potiphar.

Had Joseph never met Potiphar, he never would have gone to Potiphar's house to be accused of rape by Potiphar's wife and sent to jail. Had he not gone to jail, he would have never met the butler and the baker to interpret their dreams. Had he not interpreted their dreams, he would have never met Pharaoh, had he not met Pharaoh, he would have never interpreted Pharaoh's dreams. Had he not interpreted Pharaoh's dreams, he would have never become ruler and chief of commerce over Egypt. Had he not become ruler over

Egypt, he would have never saved a whole nation of his people. So you see, at all times God was in control of what seemed to be out of control. When the devil brings evil, God will make it good. God is in control of the devil when the devil is in control of your stuff.

Maybe it would have been better if my family had explained my conception to me. In the South, people often hid illicit relationships. The damage came, not with the truth, but with a question from the devil, which had the contents of a suggestion that made a strong statement. It was brutal when a stranger revealed it without preparation or explanation. If someone outside of your family says personal things about your family, and doesn't explain the details, it can be very damaging. God is not the author of confusion. For someone to mention that this Tom Johnson was my biological dad brought confusion, fear, and mistrust. But what was meant for evil, God turned for good.

Information from the devil binds and captures us and sends us on a destructive course. "He comes to steal, to kill, and to destroy" (John 10:10). His information has a subtle hidden message. He is crafty and can easily sneak up on you if you're not watching, or if you don't understand spiritual warfare. Watch those bearers of bad news. They can come dressed up, but on the inside they are messed up.

In my case the devil took the truth and twisted it at the wrong time to confuse my emotions that took a lifetime from which to recover. The devil loves to take your passions or emotions and misdirect them, taking fifteen or twenty years of your life on useless experiences. Before you can wake up, you are so messed up in bitterness, it will take the rest of your life to pull yourself back together.

Yes, Tom Johnson is my biological dad, but I was later informed that he never came back to Alabama. It was true that he was my dad, but it was a lie that he was in Alabama. Mr. Reuben Heard, Jr. was my stepdad, but it wasn't a stranger's business to inform me. The way it was done with its damaging affects crushed me for most of my life until Jesus turned the whole thing around and made me free.

Many of us are hurt from the history we've learned of ourselves, our parents, and other members of our families. We have fears and dislikes about each other that have caused us to dislike and sometimes to hate each other. We have become so separated that we cannot socialize with each other at family reunions. Whatever these fears and dislikes are that cause such separation, they must be brought to the feet of the Prince of Peace, Jesus Christ, Who tells us "If the son therefore shall make you free, ye shall be free indeed"(John 8:36).

I'm twelve years old, and my mother is dead at age thirty-two. I'm totally confused about who I am and why I'm in this big world without the love of a mother to which I had become accustomed. How could she leave me, and how could God allow her to leave? Certainly He could have done many things on that fateful Tuesday of her passing other than hurt me. I've come to know that God is good anyhow. Just maybe my mother was too good for Jim Crow, segregation, Ku Klux Klan, and all of the hate. Just maybe her mission was to birth five wonderful children and leave here. Like Job, I have come to say, **"The Lord gave and the Lord hath taken away; blessed be the name of the Lord" (Job 1:21).** Hopefully, once you've finished this book, you will understand some of the deep things of God and bless Him in all things.

After this woman, a woman I never saw again, devastated me with the information about my parentage, I ran home crushed. I had a new name in my life: Tom Johnson, who I was told was my daddy. How could this be? I've never heard of this man. Who is he? Where is he? And how could he be anything to me and I don't know him and have never seen him? These were questions going through my mind as I hurried up the hill to our family home. As I drew close to the house, fear and doubt set in. Who am I and what am I doing here? When I finally reached the house — and it seemed to take a lifetime to get there—the strange woman's words echoed in my mind: *"Did you see your daddy Tom Johnson when he was here from Detroit?"* I found my granddaddy, my stepfather and my Aunt Mildred all together, and I just blurted out what was told to me down the street by someone I now know was the devil himself. In those days, a child remained in a child's place. We were not to disrespect our elders. So for me to walk in and blurt out something that was told to me down the street was totally out of order.

But I needed answers to some questions that I didn't understand. And if anyone could answer me and straighten out this mess, it was the oldest member of our family, my granddad Solomon. My aunt Mildred told me to shut my mouth, which was the proper thing for me to do. But my granddaddy reluctantly began to explain to me that Mr. Heard had married my mother after I was born, and there was another person in my life named Tom Johnson who lived somewhere in Detroit.

I loved Mr. Heard, and I've never considered him to be anyone but my daddy. I built up a great dislike for Tom Johnson when I found out he had never given me one red penny. That dislike would take me to places I did not need to go, and it drove me to things that I did not need to do.

My brothers and sisters, please do not abandon our children. They are our future. They are not responsible for how they got here. We are the ones who have lain down in sin. Our children are the result of our lust, not responsible for it. We are held responsible for our stewardship over that which God has entrusted to us. And when the Master of all stewards asks us to give an account, what will we tell Him who knows all, sees all and is righteous and just in His judgement over us? In fact, we are instructed to not only bring up our children in the ways of God (Proverbs 22:6), but to leave them an inheritance (Proverbs 13:22). We can and should leave a financial inheritance and the heritage of a good education. God says a good man will leave an inheritance for his children. But the greatest inheritance to give them is Jesus Christ, who offers an inheritance of eternal life.

I enjoyed my childhood as much as possible without a mother's love. But I was hurt and confused.

When people looked at me, I felt they thought of me as a "bastard child." I concealed in my heart the hurt whenever I heard the word. It killed a part of me every time I heard it. And no one knew my pain but God.

My stepdad continued to take care of me. He added Saturday piano lessons to our weekly routine, a routine that included wonderful fishing trips in the summer. Eventually, his work and schedule took its toll, and I was sent to live with my Aunt Mildred. She had a Christian home, and there were two things I had to do: (1) go to church, and (2) go to school. I attended Shiloh Baptist Church where Mr. Heard served as a deacon along with other men in our small community of whom I learned to admire. In that way, I was able to continue looking up to strong, Christian male role models—my uncles, Mr. Heard, and other men in the community, many of whom sang in the male choir at church.

The Right Path

I continued to grow into my teenage years in the home of my Aunt Mildred who was married to Enoch Chaney, Jr. They had a son, Harold. I grew to become somewhat self-sufficient. I delivered milk before going to school and caddied on Saturdays. I had great high school teachers and was able to play on the basketball team and in the symphony orchestra, where I played the oboe. I was on the dance team, served as emcee at variety shows, and gave speeches during the assembly on Fridays when the whole senior class would come together in the auditorium. I graduated the most popular boy in my senior class of 1964.

Little Foxes

Alabama was a "dry" state. That meant there were many restrictions on the purchasing and drinking of alcohol, even though the age of Prohibition had long passed. You could not buy alcohol between Friday 5 p.m. and Sunday.

The people of my community were common people that worked all week. They took a drink of whiskey on the weekend and a little sip during weekdays. But most would go to church on Sundays. My uncles and their friends who I admired all sang in the male choir and held club meetings on Friday nights. Afterward, they would break out the bottle, have a taste, play a few hands of Bid Whist, crack some jokes and go their separate ways. No one ever got violent. I would take the little drops left in the whiskey bottles, combine them and take a sip after everyone had left. Little did I know this was the beginning of a long journey of sin. It all started from an innocent drink of whiskey in our home.

I remember dating an older lady while in high school. I met her in the club. I got so drunk at the club that I forgot and took off my jacket, revealing my 22-caliber pistol. The pistol was positioned in the small of my back. I placed it there because I had seen a character on a television program called "Tightrope," do that very same thing. I got drunk from drinking Vodka in the club, passed out and someone brought me home and laid me on my aunt's porch. The Lord was merciful to me that night. However, little did I know that television, along with the innocent men I admired, had planted a seed that would take me on a journey of sin and death. Gangster movies had a great affect on me and how I would live my life. It is the little foxes that spoil the whole vine.

> "I got so drunk at the club that I forgot and took off my jacket, revealing my 22- caliber

The Teen Years

I began to drink wine with the fellows after we left the golf course caddying on Saturdays. Then I began to hang with two older guys that could buy wine. One rainy night we got drunk, and they badly beat me. I should have known then that getting drunk was of the devil. But some of the people I admired drank, and some of them had houses where you could go on Sundays and buy a drink. I've learned that one of the guys who beat me is a bum in Brighton, Alabama. When I visited Brighton in recent years to do a revival at Shiloh where I was raised, I tried to find him so that I could lead him to the Lord.

I want to encourage you to watch what you do in front of children. Please monitor their relationships as closely as possible, especially in their teen years. That's when they are most vulnerable to the craftiness of Satan. We need to always put positive things in front of our children, teach them the facts of life, and don't take it for granted that they will automatically be okay. Teach them the ways of God and holiness, without which no man will see God.

The King Comes to Birmingham

Before graduating from Brighton High School, I had the pleasure of witnessing the greatest move of God I've ever seen in my lifetime. In those days it was understood that as a Black man you did not dare stare at a white woman. Instead we were expected to cross over to the other side of the street when approaching them. They really had us hoodwinked and bedazzled. We drank from the water fountain that specifically stated, "Colored." We ate in public places that carried the same signs to obey. We remembered to sit behind the green sign with white lettering that said, "Colored" on the public buses. I remember the Ku Klux Klan riding through our neighborhood wearing white sheets to intimidate us. The word "nigger" or "boy" or "gal" was common when referring to us. This was the overall atmosphere of Jim Crow in the state of Alabama.

One midsummer day, everything changed. There was something different about this day. There was a peace, a calm, and a quietness. We were all sitting in our classrooms. Little did we know that a quiet storm was about to happen this day at Brighton High and all over the state of Alabama.

Everyone was in his or her assigned seats, and you dared not leave until the bell rang. Our principal, Dr. Charles Allen Brown, ran a tight ship. We were basically respectful children, but children all the same. All of a sudden, someone ran down the hallway shouting, *"MARTIN LUTHER KING IS IN TOWN!"*

We forgot our inhibitions and ran like wild fire toward Birmingham, which is about eight to ten miles from Brighton. People came from everywhere, running and catching whatever mode of transportation possible to get to Birmingham. We literally left school unauthorized, not realizing we were answering a call of God. We lived in the tradition of Jim Crow, but this day we obeyed God rather than man.

I had the privilege, and I do count it a privilege, of witnessing first-hand a day that millions have seen on television: dogs unleashed on black women, men and children, who were sprayed with fire hydrant water hoses and beaten brutally. That's what we walked into when Martin came to town, and the rest is history. But the end result is unfathomable. I hear church people talk about God moving in the church, and everybody leaves church the same way in which they came. But that day, I personally saw God move. We now have seen and experienced the results of that great move of God since Martin came to town.

When God moves, there is a change of heart, mind and soul. When God moves, He changes the course of history.

Martin's Ministry

Now that I know the Lord, I can stand on His Word and say without a doubt that Dr. Martin Luther King was God-sent. He had the same Spirit that was upon Jesus, and was prophesied by the Prophet Isaiah, Chapter 61, verses1-2, and eventually fulfilled by our Lord in St. Luke 4:18 - 19, which says, "**The Spirit of the Lord is upon me, because he has anointed me to preach the gospel to the poor; He has sent me to heal the brokenhearted, to preach**

deliverance to the captives, and recovering of sight to the blind, to set at liberty them that are bruised, to preach the acceptable year of the Lord.

This same Spirit of deliverance through nonviolence that was upon Jesus was upon Dr. King. Even now, the same Spirit is delivering people.

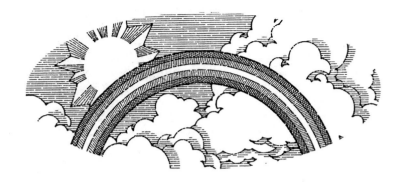

The Pimp
Satan Meets Me on Twelfth Street

L ike all too many young men in the church, the teachings of Jesus had very little effect on my moral life. I began my sexual experiences too early, beginning in my teenage years. Once a homosexual tried to pick me up while coming home from the store. On another occasion, an older woman came to my aunt's house, sat on our sofa, and spread her legs. These experiences confused me. I had just seen this older woman in the car with her boyfriend the day before.

There were other experiences as well. My high school girlfriend and I shared precious evenings together. Even though I was not faithful to her sexually, I still considered the sexual relationship to be very precious and personal. When I saw her coming out of a motel with someone else, I was hurt, even though I was in the next room with someone else! I mistakenly held to the double standard that what was good for the gander was not okay for the goose. With these illicit and confusing experiences, I subconsciously began to develop a dislike for women. As much as I was attracted to them, and needed the love from them that I longed for in my mother's absence, I also came to distrust them. I found myself searching for a love that had been abruptly taken away with the passing of my mother. I was confused for a long time. How could a woman have sex and not love the person with whom she was naked? But after all, that's how I had gotten here.

Choices

After successfully graduating from high school, my uncles, Enoch Chaney and James Calvert, sat me down and told me to pick a college. They promised to pay my way as long as I would attend. But a seed planted long ago led me to deceptively seek out this Tom Johnson in Detroit, who was supposedly my biological dad. I knew my Aunt Vera lived in Detroit and that her husband worked in an automobile factory. I decided to move to Detroit and get a job instead of going to college. This was the first big mistake of my life.

Young people go to school, get an education, make something of yourself, then let wayward fathers and mothers find you. Have mercy on them and love them with God's love. Forgive and help them, for they know not what they do.

My desire was to get a job, make some money, find this Tom Johnson and show him that I made it without him. I was told that my Aunt Vera would know where Tom lived, and that her husband, Pat Patterson, was a supervisor in the factory and would find me a job. Now the table was set for me to really begin life in the city.

My dearly beloved, "Trust in the Lord, with all thine heart, lean not to thine own understanding, but in all thy ways acknowledge Him and he shall direct thy paths" (Proverbs 3: 5-6). There is a way that seemeth right to a man, but the end thereof are the ways of death (Proverbs 14: 12).

Don't be anxious for the things of this world. When you are anxious and greedy for the world's gifts that soon disappear, the devil will meet you and misguide you. Take it from me; I've been there, done that. Things will leave you or you will leave them. I acquired many material things, only to lose them in the end; I found out that Jesus was more than enough all the time.

In June of 1964, I boarded the train for Detroit, Michigan. After boarding, I recognized Mrs. Neighbors one of my favorite elementary school teachers on the same train. That gave me a sense of security that I was headed in the right direction. After all, she was smart, pretty, on the same train, and going in the same direction. In those days teachers were our role models. I relaxed and slept with full assurance that I was on the right track and the future was very bright.

The Day I Met Tom Johnson

I arrived in Detroit, moved into my Aunt Vera's house, and got a job in the factory almost immediately, making more money than I'd ever made. The 1960's were Detroit's "Golden Years" when General Motors, Ford, and Chrysler were kings of the hill. The unions negotiated great pay and generous overtime bonuses. I bought some nice clothes, a diamond watch, and a ring.

It was during the fall season, my day off, on my way to catch the bus downtown when a stranger pulled up next to me.

"Are you Alfred Calvert?"

"Yes."

"I am your daddy, Tom Johnson. Let me have that coat!"

Tom Johnson caught me by surprise. The coat I had on was cashmere and I was totally disappointed at how he looked and at what he said. Needless to say, I did not consider giving him anything, especially my new coat. However, I was friendly and wanted to know more about him, but did not let on. He told me where he lived, which was a few blocks down the street from my Aunt Vera. I said thanks, moved on about my business. Yet, in my heart I was anxious to see him again.

Foolish Choices, More Mistakes

I was working the evening shift in the foundry at Dodge Main, located in Hamtramck, Michigan, a suburb of Detroit. A co-worker had befriended me, giving me a ride to and from work, for I had no car at that time. My co-worker and his riders would light small cigarettes that smelled bad to and from work. They called me square because I refused to smoke. There was also a young man, Tim, who lived across the street from us on Cloverlawn who sat on the porch most evenings.

> **"I took a few drags off the weed. After that, nothing, and I mean nothing, was the same."**

There were not many blacks on Cloverlawn during those days in the mid-60's.

Fresh out of Birmingham, Alabama, I knew how to dress slick. Some of the sharpest dressers in the country are from that city in the deep South. The young man took kindly to me, because I looked the part. Tim worked in his brother's barbershop; they both wore their hair processed, and I thought slick hair-dos were the thing. Tim offered me some weed one day and I accepted. I took a few drags off the weed. After that, nothing, and I mean nothing, was the same.

Later, when my associates would pass the weed to me, I didn't like it, but took it to fit in so that I could be a part of what was happening.

Young people, please don't use any drugs. Drugs are a dead end. Be careful of the company you keep. The devil was sending all types of people my way to entice, entrap, and entangle me into a life of sin that lasted over twenty years. The devil plays on our mind and emotions.

To the church: I believe that many of our youth are into piercing, tattoos, drugs, sex, and violence, because they want to be a part of something, anything, not knowing that Jesus is everything. The true church must reach out and counteract this move of Satan with the power of God, His word, sharing the salvation story.

In 1965, Twelfth Street, (now Rosa Parks Boulevard) was a one-way street with trick houses and nightclubs like Club 12, the spot bar, where pimps and players hung out, and places to eat like Hughes Barbecue. There were places like *Benny Mullins Barbershop* to get your hair processed. It was a bustling street, full of legal and illegal activities. At Club 12, pimps parked in new Fleetwood and Eldorado Cadillacs with the motors running and beautiful girls clad in skimpy tight wares on every corner with love for sale. You could hear the cry for quick cash from the lips of prostitutes as the chirp of birds chirping for food.

"Pull over honey; ten and two baby."

The ten was for the loving and two was for the room in the trick house.

My first night on Twelfth Street came unexpectedly when the gentleman with whom I rode to and from work stopped there to purchase some dope. I did not know this at the time, but since I've matured in life and learned the games people play, the Lord has shown me that this was the fatal trip that led me deep into sin and death. It came so quickly and easily that I didn't even have time to think about it.

It was on a Thursday night, and we had just gotten paid. We cashed our checks, and on our way home, he parked on Twelfth Street. So much was going on. Ladies were bent over in cars, flagging cars down, running to and from cars. White men were going into doorways with black women, and women were standing in doorways pointing to their crotches and throwing kisses as men passed by. Here I was from the South; I had never been in the bright lights and big city and would not have known a prostitute if you gave me one. This was bigger than life to me. I was mesmerized.

I was excited when I saw black men driving the most elegant Cadillacs I'd ever seen. They were parked along the street, sitting in fine cars with their processed hair, and some would have hats cocked to the side on top of the processed hair. I loved what I saw. I was attracted to the street life and distracted from God.

Here I was, dressed in a filthy Dodge Main blue uniform with foundry dust all over me. Yet I knew that I could go home and come back looking just like the men that drove the pretty Cads.

> "The place upstairs was the weed house where the ladies would take their tricks for the 'ten and two.'"

Mr. Metcalf, in whose car I was riding, knew I had never been in this environment. When he stopped in front of the building, he asked me if I wanted to follow him upstairs. Blindly, I followed him into that dark and dreary place.

The place upstairs was the weed house where the ladies would take their tricks for the "ten and two." I'd never had an experience with a prostitute, so when the young lady who looked to be about three years younger than I was asked me if I wanted to date, I thought she liked me. I had no idea she only desired money. My few experiences with a woman giving her body to me had nothing to do with me paying for it.

She wore glasses and had smooth brown skin. She had a pretty face and was well built. The excitement of lying in bed with a pretty stranger set in and I gave her the ten and two. She told me if I gave her five more I could have *half and half*–half oral and half intercourse. I gave her the five dollars. After we finished, she talked about how badly my foundry clothes smelled. My heart was cut to the core.

I watched her as she cleaned herself, went down

stairs and gave something to a black man sitting in a green Fleetwood Cadillac. He wore dark glasses at night, and his hat was cocked to the side. I watched him as he sat there counting money. I felt bad paying for something and being treated so rudely afterward.

I despaired when I found out that I had done what was called, "turning a trick." The thought of her giving the money to the man siting in the Fleetwood frustrated me. I made up my mind that night that I would be on the receiving end of the cash, and no woman would ever talk to me rudely again in life. That night, I purposed in my heart that I was going to drive the Fleetwood, and women would give me their money. This was the life for me, not some dirty factory. I would never again be told how bad my clothes smelled. Someday, I would receive the love from women that these great men were getting, well dressed and siting in their pretty cars. From that night until thirty years later, I searched for love in all the wrong places, until God came into my heart.

I had already bought myself fine clothes and jewelry. I would eventually get my hair processed and pursue this life filled with sex and money. The spirit of deception, temptation, lust, confusion, hurt, false love, and false satisfaction pulled me into its web that night and the venom flowed through my being leading me to death. Satan had planted the spirit of corruption.

I saw much in that short night. Now I understand the temptation our Lord felt in **Luke 4:5** which reads, **"And the devil taking Him (Jesus) up into a high** *mountain, showed unto Him all the kingdoms of the world in a moment of time."*

In less than forty-five minutes, I saw pimps, money, prostitutes, oral sex, Cadillacs, dope, trick houses, liquor, diamonds, and it all fascinated me to the point where my curiosity would not rest until I became a part of it.

Satan knows we are all born into sin (**Romans 5:12**) through the first man, Adam. The enemy watches us from birth and takes advantage of our sin nature by dangling in front of us whatever we long for or are attracted to according to our flesh. If you like to drink and drive, he'll put you in a fast car and give you too much alcohol to drink so that you can kill yourself. He knew I desired a woman's love, because my mother had passed at an early age just as I was getting attached to her. He knew I loved to make money, so he showed me the woman making and giving the money to a man, which caused me to think that she must love the man. It was deception in the first degree. Satan used money and women in his attempts to lure me to hell.

Satan was waiting for me that night on Twelfth Street. He flashed everything he knew I liked before my eyes in a moment of time, and I was messed up for over thirty years. It began with drops of whiskey and a puff of marijuana. It is the little foxes that spoil the vine. A little fox is too small to reach the top of the vine, so it chews at the root of the vine until it dies. That's how sin does us in our lives. It begins with a little drink at an innocent card game. Then comes more whiskey and the weed, and before you realize it you are trying cocaine and heroin.

Nightlife in Motown

Eventually I moved away from my Aunt Vera's into my own apartment on the corner of Dexter and Fullerton. In 1965, those were very nice apartments. I was told that the "Queen of Soul," Aretha Franklin, lived in the one that I had occupied. By this time, one of the boss pimps, "Will C.," lived in the building. There were two call girls, a pimp, "Fat Larry," and a very nice gentleman who became my friend named Ivy Hunter who worked at Motown.

Positive Impact

Ivy and I became running buddies. We began to hang out. He would take me down on West Grand Boulevard to "Hitsville U.S.A.," Berry Gordy's operation that birth Motown. I began to meet some of the Motown recording artists. It was a pleasure to meet and be in the company of such talented people. We listened to the Four Tops' song, "Ask The Lonely," one night in Ivy's suite before they dubbed the lyrics to the music. I also had the pleasure of meeting Wanda Rogers of the Marvellettes while at his home. It was love at first sight for me! The people I met like The Temptations, Stevie Wonder, Marvin Gaye, Norman Whitfield, and many others were very pleasant people. These were probably my best memories of that era.

I visited my high school in the 80's, and some of my old teachers told me they always thought I would host my own television program, and that they looked for me to be in the movies. Just maybe God was trying to show me my real self when He allowed me to meet the positive people at Motown. But the seed of pimps and prostitutes was planted deep in my soul.

We would frequent the "Twenty Grand" nightclub together. Because I was hanging out with Ivy, we would go to the front of the long line, get inside for free, and enjoy the shows. I was privileged to hear the great Chuck Jackson sing, "Any Day Now," and other stars including Billy Steward, Joe Tex, and members of the Motown gang.

The after hour clubs in those days were the "in" places to be after the regular clubs closed. *"Men love darkness, rather than light, because their deeds are evil" (John3:19)*. It was in the after hour places where pimps and prostitutes hung out, drinking, snorting cocaine, and smoking weed. It was here that the seed of darkness was deeply planted in my life, and I was more than ever determined to become one of the night people.

The devil magnified himself through the night people. We would sit at the bar drinking and snorting cocaine, and suddenly one of the players would say something very clever, like, *"If I fell dead right now the undertaker would not have to dress me because I'm already sharp."* I'd never had so much fun.

The pimps and players were dressed in some of the prettiest tailored suits, 'gator shoes, custom jewelry, with wavy, processed hair, manicured nails, and four pockets full of money. You could not tell me that this was not the life. The prostitutes were sexy with their short dresses or hot pants, with their long legs and no panty hose. There were all kinds of moves going down. The one who had the "blow" (cocaine) was the most important man of the house. Now and then someone would come through with some beautiful, "hot" (stolen) clothes or jewels.

Often a "loose" prostitute, (one without a man), would choose a pimp right there in the after hour joint by giving him the money she made that night. Or, a loose prostitute would get high and give you the sign that she just wanted to go and have some fun in a motel, and she would pay.

In *Ezekiel 28:13*, God says, *"Every precious stone was thy (Satan's) covering, the sardius, topaz, and the diamond, the beryl, the onyx, and the jasper, the sapphire, the emerald and the carbuncle, and gold."* Satan is a master in flash, and in making his children appear to be more than they are. He's the master of illusion and will go to any extreme to cover us with fine material things, only to lead us to hell. He will make you think that you can have any or all of these precious coverings, but as soon as he entangles you he will take them back and leave you to die like a fool. Trust me, he will send one of his thieves to steal, to kill, and to destroy you. He will take back all he loaned you for a season and give it to the next fool to lead them to hell.

In *Ezekiel 28:15*, God says: *"Thou wast perfect in thy ways from the day that thou wast created, till iniquity was found in thee."* Satan is the master of making one feel perfectly satisfied in iniquity, or lawlessness, or sin.

I must take this time to thank God. When we accept Jesus Christ as Lord and Savior, we are all children of light and of the day, and not of the night, nor of darkness, therefore let us not sleep as do others, but let us watch and be sober (*I Thessalonians 5: 5-6*).

There are a couple of things I can say about people in "the life," the night people: (1) they stick together, and (2) they will help each other. But then Jesus did say, *"For the children of this world are in their generation wiser than children of light." (Luke: 16: 8)*. My experience in Christendom thus far is we really don't have the closeness Christ intended for us to have. To be all baptized into one Body, by one Spirit, we should realize that we have much more in common. We should be able to just get along. Then again, I guess we are all so busy going to Heaven that we don't have time for each other. Some of us speak in tongues, but won't speak to the person sitting next to us in the pews. It is the devil's job to keep us confused and separated, and he is very good at what he does.

Satan has blinded the eyes of the people of darkness, who often call themselves people in "the life." I remember the saying, *"I love the life I live, and I live the life I love."* In all actuality, we were all on our way to eternal death without Christ. We thanked the pimp-god when a prostitute would bring home a bundle of money. We thought the pimp-god had smiled down on us. Satan has the night people in "the life" deceived with the glitter of money and possessions. Greed in some instances can lead to death, because the more you get, the more you want. Even the night people who don't use drugs shop excessively for clothes and jewels. It is always more, more, and more.

When someone hosted a big party or we all showed up at the championship fight, we had to outshine the other. Night people are the best at putting a three hundred dollar hat, two-thousand dollar suit, thousand dollar shoes, and ten-thousand dollars worth of jewels on a hell-bound body whose sin-sick state isn't worth a dime.

The Basic Character of Satan

It is the character of Satan to appear beautiful. After all, he was created the most beautiful angel in Heaven. After he lost his position, he did not lose his ability to counterfeit or to falsify. It is very important for us to know in detail the character and personality of Satan in order to avoid being ignorant of his devices and strategies. Let's look at some verses in the book of Ezekiel, where God moved the author to describe Satan's status in Heaven.

Ezekiel 28:13: Thou hast been in Eden, the garden of God. Because Satan has been so close to God, he knows how to counterfeit the things of God. When a counterfeiter knows his trade, he can be very sneaky in his attempt to fool us. A counterfeit hundred-dollar bill can look so much like the real bill. One must be very vigilant to catch the nuance of difference. It takes an expert with a magnifying glass to make the distinction. If we don't have Jesus, the Expert Who spoiled principalities and powers and made a show of them openly when He rose from the dead to overcome all the powers of Satan, even death, we'll never be able to avoid Satan's traps. When we don't put Jesus first in our lives, the power of death from Satan will beat down our self-esteem, our hopes for tomorrow, our emotions, and our positive thoughts. When we don't have the Holy Spirit for our magnifier to teach us all things and guide us into all truth, we can easily be deceived by the counterfeit.

The Scriptures tell us in *Ezekiel 28:14: "Thou art the anointed cherub that covereth. And I have set thee so. Thou wast upon the holy mountain of God."* Satan was dapper! He was well dressed with the power of God. He is accustomed to the heights; he knows how to use his power of illusion to make us feel that we are on top of the world. You cannot tell a pimp with three to five women working for him, bringing money to him every three to five hours each day, that he is not on top of the world. You cannot tell a dope dealer who is counting shoeboxes or grocery bags full of money daily that he or she is not on top of the world, especially with all of the sex and recognition that comes with it. Look at the rest of this verse in **Ezekiel 28:14:** *"Thou hast walked up and down in the midst of the stones of fire."*

Satan will use precious stones to take us up and then to bring us down. Diamonds, gold, and precious things are his forte. Satan will give you all the flash you want. He knows how to deceive us, to make us think we are better than others, because we have more than others or because we think we fit into a higher class. We are blind to the fact that Jesus Christ is the light of the world, and shining for Him is all the shine we need. Shining for Jesus is the only shine that will last. When we die we cannot take any worldly riches with us. The Bible says, *"All they that be fat (rich) upon earth shall eat and worship, and all they that go down to the dust of the earth (die) shall bow before him and none can keep alive his own soul" (Psalm 22:29).* What would it profit you to gain the whole world and lose your soul?

Allow me to minister to you a bit more about the real character and nature of the devil as written in the Bible. I need you to understand that the forces which were working against me are the same forces that are working against us now. *Ezekiel 28:16: "By the multitude of thy merchandise they have filled the midst of thee with violence, and thou hast sinned."*

By the multitude of merchandise—violence, dope, guns in the wrong hands, abortions, alcohol, crack, spousal abuse, child abuse, pornography, child pornography–you name it, Satan's got it. All of these things create violence and they are sin, and this is just a small taste of his merchandise. Now look at what else God tells him in **Ezekiel 28:16: "I will cast thee as profane out of the mountain of God, and I will destroy thee, O covering cherub from the midst of the stones of fire."**

If God cast out Satan as profane (defined as "impure or defiled," or "to treat something sacred with abuse"), what do we think He will do to us when we follow the world and the ways of Satan? I'm in no way inferring that we should not desire or have precious stones, but we cannot make them our God. We should not sin to gain or to keep material things. When you are transformed, changed from children of the night into children of the light and day, you must remain sober and watchful.

In closing this portion on the character of Satan, we look at **Ezekiel 28:17**: **"Thine heart was lifted up because of thy beauty."**

Have you ever noticed that some of the most beautiful women in the world are strippers and play-boy bunnies? I've never seen an ugly call girl! Most professional prostitutes are good looking. The male dancers and strippers are well-built and handsome men who sell their souls for fame and fortune that will pass away. They cannot take any of the fame or fortune to the grave with them! It's appointed to man once to die and then the judgment. Our bodies are to be living sacrifices, holy unto God.

God also told Satan further in ***Ezekiel 28:17,*** ***"Thou hast corrupted thy wisdom by reason of thy brightness, I will cast thee to the ground, I will lay thee before kings, that they may behold thee."*** Many unsaved entertainers meet kings and queens, but what spirit do they have? The Scriptures also remind us in ***Proverbs 16:25: "There is a way that seemeth right to a man, but the end thereof are the ways of death."***

Today Satan has blinded the eyes of many to think that drugs are the ultimate fulfillment, the solution to their empty hearts, when it is leading them to death and family destruction. Many are deceived by the temporary thrill of sexual relationships, when it can so easily result in the worst ills. Many have been cut down by the AIDS demon, the natural result of living contrary to God's laws. They lay down in a thrill and they come up with an ill.

Satan has people taking abortion lightly. In the judgment, I believe the souls of aborted babies will come face to face with those who killed the flesh of the baby. God said, ***"Before I formed thee in the belly I knew thee" (Jeremiah 1: 5)***. If God formed it and knew it before it was formed, that makes it wrong for us to kill it. But he made a way of escape for the unborn baby, because all souls belong to God. We can kill the body, but only God can kill the soul (***Matthew10:28***).

My friends, those of you whom God has led to pick up this book, the Bible says in ***I Corinthians 1: 21: "For after that in the wisdom of God the world*** *by wisdom knew not God, it pleased God by the foolishness of preaching to save them that believe."* All of you beautiful people who are hung up on your bodies to make money and don't use your bodies to glorify God who made the body are in trouble at the judgment if you refuse to believe in the death, burial, and resurrection of Jesus Christ, Who came to save the soul. God understands that the preaching of the cross is foolishness to you now, but I'm encouraging you to: *"Seek the Lord while he may be found, call upon him while he is near. Let the wicked forsake his way and the unrighteous man his thoughts. Let him return unto the Lord and he will have mercy on him and to our God, for he will abundantly pardon"* *(Isaiah 55:6-7).*

My beloved, the flesh will perish and go back to the dust of the earth from which it came. Teeth will fall out, hair will turn gray, skin will wrinkle and become unattractive, but the soul must live somewhere. God made the soul a living soul and only God can kill what he has made alive. I appeal to all of the night people, especially my old pimp buddies who knew me as "Big Al Chavallo" or "One Leg Al." Many of you across this country know how I served the same devil you are serving faithfully. It is pure deception to take all of you to hell forever, and forever is a long time to spend anywhere, especially in outer darkness.

I thank God that *"I once was blind, but now I see."* You can see also if you will pray this simple prayer with all your heart.

PRAYER

Have mercy upon me Oh God, according to your loving kindness. Please erase everything I've done wrong according to the multitude of your tender mercies. I have sinned against you, and against you only have I sinned. I believe that you died and rose again on the third day. Wash me in the blood of Jesus and make me clean. Create in me a clean heart Oh God, and renew within me a right spirit. Then lead me to the water to be baptized in Jesus' name and fill and seal me with your precious Spirit. In Jesus' name. Amen.

Born A Bastard, Now Born Again

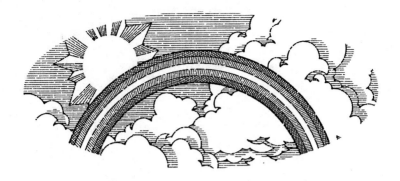

West Side Experience

I was always well dressed and well accepted among the people of the night. For a while, I continued to work at Dodge Main, building my wardrobe so I could fit in with the big time players and pimps of the night. I had begun to ride with another Chrysler worker who recently had moved into my apartment complex on Dexter and Fullerton. We would smoke weed and drink beer and wine at his house before going to work for the evening shift.

I made the grave mistake of allowing one of his friends, along with his wife, into my apartment. This "friend of a friend" used his wife as a decoy to case my place for a break-in while I was at work. This guy stole everything I owned. The thought that a friend of a friend would break into my home was totally foreign to me. In Alabama, things were so different. We left our door open, and a neighbor could come in and borrow milk or eggs when no one was home. I went into a state of shock when I came home that night and found my place violated. The devil will set you up with his own wife.

The drinking and smoking had caught up with me. I was laid off from work at Dodge Main. I had just a few nice things left in the cleaners after the break-in. I had a few fronts, but now I had to use them to look impressive to keep up with my "friends" in the nightlife. Without a job, I had to cop, (get a prostitute to choose me) and really make it in the nightlife.

I lost my apartment. I had become careless in my personal affairs due to drinking and getting high. The after hour joints became my second home. After that the street life swallowed me up quickly. The whole world around me began to change. Even my location changed from the west side to the east side.

Despite my poverty and state of no direction, I remember striving to keep up my appearance. One day, as I decided to go for a walk down Charlevoix, a good looking, middle-aged woman driving a new Fleetwood drove up beside me with the prettiest smile and asked me where was I going. Little did she know that I was broke and hungry with no direction in my life.

She picked me up and brought me to the west side of Detroit to a gorgeous apartment, where once again I succumbed to the temptation of sex and alcohol. In the middle of the night, the woman woke me and gave me cab fare back to the east side. I remember being very disappointed. I thought I had caught me a free ride for a time. Remember, I had developed a pimp mentality. I had a choice to spend the cab fare or get to the east side another way. I managed to prolong my stay by giving her more sex.

Years later, after I'd gotten myself together I saw her going into the Joe Louis Arena. As soon as I approached her, she looked directly into my eyes and clutched the hand of the older gentleman. It appeared as though the three of us knew something, but no one said a word. I went on my way confused at why she had taken me home and made love to me the way she did and never tried to see me again. We could not even speak to each other.

> "I had become careless in my personal affairs due to drinking and getting high. The after hour joints were my second home."

After our one-night-stand, she dropped me off at a restaurant on Linwood, *"The Green Leaf Cafe,"* which at that time had the best food in the city. It was there that I met one of my best friends in life. Even at this very moment I have a tear in my eye just thinking of my friend William Herring, the Black Nigerian, better known as Bronco.

I was sitting at the counter in *The Green Leaf Cafe.* My breakfast was being prepared. I ordered sausage, grits, eggs, and the best biscuits in town. In walked this well-groomed gentleman, with a complexion as black as the ace of spades. He was very neatly dressed; his hair was processed to the bone. He talked very loud, and he was friendly to all the ladies. It appeared that everybody knew him. There was an old saying in those days, *"Game recognizes game."* We instantly recognized each other and immediately became the most trusted friends. Little did we know on that morning that we would become friends for over thirty years, and that the Lord would use me some thirty years later to convert Bronco to Jesus just long enough for Bronco to grow strong in the Lord before the Lord would call him home.

It's experiences like this that assures me the Lord is alive and real.

After we had breakfast and jived with all of the waitresses, we drove by his flat where he picked up some money, and we headed to the east side. We laughed and talked all the way as if we had known each other all of our lives. In fact, when he got ready to take me home, he went inside with me to meet some of my friends: Jerome, Johnny Williams the brother of Paul Williams of the Temptations, Bobby, and Keith. Bronco waited for me as I cleaned myself up, and we continued to ride for the rest of the day.

Bronco was a numbers man, and part of his route was on the east side. It was exciting to watch him come back to the car and count the money people had given him to play their numbers. At the close of the day we would stop by a lady friend of his, and she would cook us a full course meal. She had a girl friend upstairs who was sexy and had no man. As Bronco would hang downstairs, I would go upstairs until the next morning. Or, all of us went to the club where his girl worked as a barmaid and drank free of charge. *"Now,"* I thought, *"I'm back in the life."*

Bronco was a good hustler and a gentleman. We bonded as running buddies. He literally began to take care of me on a daily basis. I would ride with him picking up numbers, go to the race track to play the horses, and sometimes I won, because his Mob friend would tell him which horse would win the race. We played golf daily.

Bronco had a knack for managing after hour joints. He was the boss and I was his best friend. It was in his after hour joint where I began to meet people who respected me. They looked up to me because they did not know what my position was. All they knew was that I was well-dressed and Bronco's partner. I met a square girl in the after hours club who fell in love with me and began to take care of me. She was the nicest girl in the world, but I was a fool.

The square girl taking care of me was confirmation from the devil that I could pimp. However, the real pimps had ladies on the street corner. My ultimate goal was to have some *"mud-kickers"* (street corner prostitutes) as they were called, working for me.

It was through Bronco that I began to meet the players on the west side of Detroit, and I was accepted as one of the night people. It was a strange thing how a sharp hairdo, pinkie ring, and clothes could project a winning image in this nightlife we called "the life." Even professionals could make a good impression. But, when you get to know them over a few drinks, you'll find the real person. We all have issues that are revealed when people get really close to us. The Bible says, ***"The heart is deceitful above all things and desperately wicked, who can know it? I the Lord" (Jeremiah 17: 9).***

Appearance can be the greatest illusion. That's why we are so surprised when someone famous or very notable commits suicide or is caught with drugs, or is discovered engaging in some other immoral act. However, know for a surety that there is something wrong with all of us. There is none righteous, no, not one. We all need Jesus who knew no sin, but was made sin that we might be made the righteousness of God in him (***II Corinthians 5:21***). Man is the unrighteous one who on the outside is dressed up, but on the inside is messed up.

We hung out in Bronco's after hour club one night. Traffic was slow. In walked two nurses looking for something to get into. They had a couple of drinks and played a game called craps (dice). Men "in the life" (pimps) love prostitutes. But more than that, they love the pleasure of square girls coming into their midst. It's like a little lamb falling into the hands of a wolf. We were hoping the square girls were not so innocent after all. And sometimes we were right. I have found in my lifetime that some square ladies like the same men that prostitutes like, because they are looking for excitement in their lives. We kept the excitement real live!

To the ladies who are known by street people as "squares": Before you get excited about some good-looking, well-dressed, dapper guy, get excited about Jesus Christ. Without Him there will always be a void in your life that only God can fill. Some women look to men who are well dressed, drive pretty cars, wear nice jewels, and keep plenty of money, because everyone loves a winner. That's human nature.

Men of stature appear to have power. Woman came from man and it's common for her to seek power. What she is not aware of is that men who are "in the life" and out of Christ have a false power, a deceptive power. Real power is in the Holy Ghost, not in the abundance of things. Pimps and players selfishly love the square women who enters into their lives. They don't know how to love them with the love of God. They are lost and dead in sin themselves.

I began to hang out on the west side of Detroit. I was befriended by a "boss player," named Westside. I met Baby R., Harry C., and others, and we all hung out on Twelfth Street at the Chit Chat Lounge. That's where I met Westside's sister who was a street prosti-tute, call girl, thief, and a very attractive lesbian. The devil sent me four demons in one woman. The sister chose me the first night she saw me. I was well dressed in a double-breasted, forest green blazer and mint green pants with a green knit sweater trimmed in white and some white sandals. My hair was very long and laid with the process called the "Tony Curtis." We always sat at the corner of the bar where all the ladies passed on their way to the rest room. While everyone else drank shots of whisky, we purchased the bottle of Cognac and sat it on the bar so the ladies would know drinks were no problem.

The attractive, young woman approached me and asked me to dance. While dancing, she moved her mid-section very close to me. After the dance she followed me to the bar. I allowed her to sit while I stood. She pulled me close and kissed me. My partner, west side, came over and introduced her to me."

Lawiss (my street name), *have you met my sister?"* Satan had just sent me my first real prostitute. I had acquired the street name of "Lawiss" from my best friend Bronco, who had read a book about a man who would get physically ill at the thought of work. Somehow, Lawiss had interpreted the dream of a king of his country and was so greatly rewarded that he never worked the rest of his life. Bronco knew I hated work with a passion so he named me, *"The Great Lawiss."*

Westside's sister gave me a trap (money), went downtown to a shoe store and bought me a pair of green alligator shoes. She and Westside's lady flew to Canada, checked into a hotel and tricked with members of a hockey team. A week later, they came home with much Canadian money.

The deception was that I thought I had found real love even though I was in the process of becoming a boss pimp. Just "show me the money." The girls flew back to Canada and were arrested as soon as they touched down, although they were wearing wigs to disguise themselves.

Westside's sister called me late one night, inviting me to the Hotel Sheraton Cadillac downtown Detroit. I entered the smoke-filled suite where people were coupled. I couldn't make out the gender of the couples because of the dimness and smoke. She led me into another part of the suite where another young lady with a "butch" haircut was sitting on the bed.

Westside's sister took a joint of weed from between her breast and gave it to the butch girl. I was ready to leave. I had already been exposed to her making love to a woman. But I knew she had money for me, so I held my peace. She tried to entice the unattractive woman to service me sexually, but the young lady refused. I was pleased. Her interest was in my lesbian woman. My lady gave me my money, and we fooled around. I left the hotel confused about the lifestyle of the woman I cared for. However, her willingness to share sex and money assured me she loved me.

Now I was all messed up. I was sleeping with Westside's sister and other women, sometimes two women at the same time. Lucifer had control of my life. Satan will always work through your flesh: the desire of your eyes, the lust of your flesh, and any pride in your life. ***Galatians 5: 19*** says, ***"Now the works of the flesh are manifest, which are these; adultery, fornication, uncleanness, lasciviousness."***

I was in my early twenties when I caught my first prostitute. I learned to deeply care for this woman. But I have also learned that any woman who brings her money home to a man after selling her body all day or night is dead and sick in sin. Any man who waits on the woman to bring the money home depending on her for his livelihood is more sick and more dead in sin than she is. Our lives were controlled by demons from hell.

> "I was in my early twenties when I caught my first prosti-tute."

I saw her again in 1997, I was on my way to minister to some inmates at a halfway house. She was on her way to a Moorish Science meeting with a young white girl trailing behind. She was dressed as a Muslim. We passed each other as two ships in the night.

I preached the gospel at my meeting like never before. I'm sure she heard the Word for her meeting was next to ours. I know the Lord blessed, because His Word will not return void. I misused her in the pimp game a long time ago. I pray that she heard the

Word and heeded the call of God to be used by Him.

My dearly beloved brothers and sisters, please abstain from group orgies, for this is sin before God. You know this. I don't need to tell you that pleasure is fleeting and can never be fully satisfied. Learn to present your bodies as a living sacrifice. Keep yourself holy and acceptable before God, for this is what you should do at the bare minimum (See Romans 12:1-2). This is actually your real purpose in life so that God Almighty can show Himself through you to help others. Satan appeals to our flesh, and the flesh is on its way back to the dust of the earth. Get saved, and be strong in the Lord in your spirit man that will live forever.

False Power

Look in the book of Acts 8:9 and you'll see a man in "the life," a pimp, dope dealer back in those times with false power that people sought after. You will see in Acts 8: 4-8 where Philip, who had the real power of God, was preaching and people were getting healed and delivered in the city of Samaria. There was great joy in that city.

In Acts 8:9, we find a certain man called Simon who used sorcery to attract the people and to earn his living. The word *"sorcery"* in the Greek is *"pharmkeia."* We get our words *"pharmacy,"* or *"drug dispenser"* from that word. *"Pharmakon,"* another related word in the Greek, means a *drug;* a spell-giving potion; a poisoner or a magician.

In the book of Acts, Simon was a pharmakon who bewitched the people of Samaria, presenting himself as some "great one." The average pimp with a dope sack today is looked up to as some great guy, but he is really selling false hope and joy to those who believe in him.

The Bible says in **Acts 8:10** that everyone from the least to the greatest *"declared this man is the great power of God."* Any woman from the least to the

greatest could buy their drugs from Simon. Young women, poor women, old women, and rich women could go by his house and get their fix. And in the eleventh verse it says, *" . . . and to him they had regard."* They respected and looked up to him, because for a long time he had bewitched them with sorceries . . . *pharmakon* . . . drugs. We are all trying to fill a void in our lives that only Jesus can fill with His great salvation.

They looked up to Simon as if he had the power of God. But his power was false, the same false power people are looking for today when they look anywhere but to Jesus. Continue to read *verses 12 and 13* and you'll see that Simon believed and was baptized in the name of Jesus. That's what you should do today if you are not saved. If you are reading this book and know you have that dope sack giving out false hope to people, I say to you: what good would it profit you to gain the whole world and lose your soul before God, Who will judge us for all our deeds, both good and evil?

I met a square lady who was a nurse; she looked up to me because of false power. We moved into our own apartment. She was very kind to me, bringing home her paycheck on her lunch hour and buying me diamonds, a floor model TV, and a tape recorder. I remember having some peace within myself, sitting, listening and recording the Swinger, Jack Springer program.

I always wanted to be a disc jockey. I fought her for no reason at all because I had a bad spirit. I wish I could tell her today how sorry I am. My beloved, it is good to be saved and have the love of God shed abroad in our hearts by the Holy Ghost.

I have learned that selfishness and jealousy are bad spirits, which are of the devil. A man should never strike a woman, and I mean never! Can you imagine how many of us have cursed a woman or hit her, or how many families are dysfunctional today because of unnecessary fights?

Brother, sometimes the woman is having PMS, or some type of natural change in her body. It has nothing to do with another man. Don't beat her because of what you assume through jealousy. If you have this bad spirit, get saved and practice the fruit of the Holy Spirit that God will give to you after you accept His Son Jesus. Then you can practice the virtues of God.

Please allow me to give to you a formula for true success in your relationships. This is the "fruit" of the Spirit as described in **Galatians 5:22-23** that presents the following:

Love: A caring and seeking for the highest good of another person without motive for personal gain.

Joy: The feeling of gladness based on the love, grace, blessings, promises, and nearness of God that belongs to those who believe in Christ.

Peace: The quietness of heart and mind based on the knowledge that all is well between the person and God.

Longsuffering: Endurance, patience, being slow to anger or despair.

Gentleness: Not wanting to hurt someone or give him or her pain.

Goodness: Zeal for truth and righteousness and a hatred for evil.

Faith: Faithfulness, firm and unswerving loyalty and adherence to a person to whom one is united by promise, commitment, trust, and honesty.

Meekness: Restraint coupled with strength and courage; it describes a person who can be angry when anger is needed and humbly submissive when submission is needed.

Temperance: Having control or mastery over one's own desires and passions, including faithfulness to one's marriage vows.

There are no restrictions on the lifestyle indicated. There is no law prohibiting the practice and use of these virtues over and over again. You will never find a law that will convict you for living these principles.

Bad Seed Brings Bad Harvest

The devil planted a bad seed in me as I observed the character of the pimps and players while sitting in the after hour clubs. I watched their mannerisms and listened to their language. They spoke of keeping the whores "in line" by beating them. Listening to other pimp's talk of how to treat a whore led me to feel justified in beating a woman with a clothes hanger.

I was raised in a good Christian home. I have never seen a woman in my family hit by anyone. The Bible says evil communication corrupts good manners (*I Corinthians 15:33*). The writer believes that "bad communication" in the music and television programs our young people are listening to and watching corrupts them. Is there hope? Yes! It's in the Lord.

What do you think is causing the violence in our young society today? Who ever heard of a black man raping a little child? Why do brothers drive by and shoot innocent people? Why are so many young couples killing each other? We need a society check! Check out the latest video games that teach our youth to kill.

Let's check our society in with the Lord. He is our only hope. There is no fault found in Him. He is able to keep us from falling and present us faultless before His presence with exceeding joy.

I feel bad to this day concerning the way I have abused the women in my life. Even with this curse, I continued to seek the perfect love from a woman, as I continued to miss the love of my mother. But when we are dead in sin, Satan controls our lives.

My life as a pimp and petty hustler in the city of Detroit was soon to come to a close. The Feds were on me for draft dodging. I had teamed up with a gentleman by the name of Westside. I had pimped his sister and a few others, including a *"booster"* (women who shoplift daily), who would fence the clothes, selling them all to one person. I was at the heyday of my petty pimping career. Westside and I dressed up every day, processed hair and all.

One day we stopped by Texas Slim's house, another Mack. I came face to face with the same prostitute who serviced me that first fateful night on Twelfth Street before I had became a pimp. Then I remembered it was Slim sitting in the new green Fleetwood that night. I was one of them now, and of course, she did not recognize me. I looked so different, dressing out of some of the best stores in the city, wearing diamonds on my wrists and fingers. In fact, in contrast to the way she talked to me that first night with my old auto worker's uniform, she held her head down in respect of my presence. The women who prostituted themselves in those days were trained to act that way. If she got caught staring at another pimp, it could be mistaken that she had eyes for him, and this could cost her a smack in the face by her pimp or worse.

Compound Confusion

When in sin we have no moral direction, but feel as if we are on top of things. I honestly thought my friend Westside and I were having the best time of our lives, riding in his convertible, smoking weed, running in and out of the clubs drunk, pimping, and accepting money from women daily. The mere fact his sister liked women was acceptable because sin appeared exciting to have two woman in bed at the same time. I guess longing for the love I missed from my mother caused me to accept women on their terms. As long as they gave me sex and money, I believed they loved me.

I know now it's all because of sin, but when you are young and dead in sin, there is no direction in life. Who else but Satan would send a very feminine woman that I really cared for into my home, have her give me her money and sex, and then suddenly have her come home one day dressed as a man. I am ashamed to confess I took an iron pipe that secured our door and tried to break her neck with it. This was

one of the worst things that ever happened to me
emotionally. Satan was pulling me deeper into hell.
She called the police, and they locked me up. A fixer
named Harry secured my release. A fixer is a lawyer
who has power in the legal system. I went to live
with my Aunt Vera only to find out that the Feds were
looking for me for dodging the draft. I was so out of
tune with the world I didn't know what the draft was.
I lived in the underworld in total darkness, dead in
trespasses and in sin.

My soul was now steeped in that life. What or who
could deliver me?

I continued my relationship with Westside. He
would come by and pick me up at my Aunt Vera's
house. We continued to ride daily, resting and dressing, slamming convertible doors, pimping
whores, and doing drugs. I explained what had happened to me and his sister, and he understood. He
loved her, but he loved the pimp game more.

1967: How the Riots Began

The day before the riots in Detroit, Westside and I
had done the usual getting the car washed, shoes
shined, smoking weed, and playing the women. We
hung for a while that day, hit a few clubs that night
and finally decided to visit an after hours joint that
we had never frequented before. It was on Twelfth
Street near Clairmount. We were accustomed to after
hour raids. The police would raid a joint every now
and then to make things look good downtown. The
plain clothes police would come to pick up an

envelope (bribe) and leave just before the raid. They would send a "paddy wagon," take all the men downtown and let the women go free. We snorted cocaine in the paddy wagon on the way to the police station. After being fingerprinted, we paid $27.50, bailed out, and went to breakfast or our separate ways.

But this particular night, for some strange reason, the police were either drunk or a rookie was not properly instructed. Maybe some red neck who hated blacks took things a little too serious. For some strange reason the police came with a different attitude and roughed up some of the prostitutes. One of the ladies jumped off the back porch causing a stick to be driven through her leg.

The brothers who saw the incident began to break windows and loot the pawnshops on Twelfth Street. By noon that same day, most of the city of Detroit was on fire. Thus, became the riots of 1967.

I was there that morning, in the place where it all began. Now that I'm saved and know my Bible, in **John 10:10,** it tells us that, *"The thief cometh not but for to steal, to kill, and to destroy."* I understand that riots and looting are activities from Satan himself. I know who started the confusion, and God is not the author of it.

Westside and I were pimps, not thieves. We stood across the street and watched as the brothers stole. How dare we get our hands dirty breaking into windows, taking the chance that we might get cut and bleed all over our pretty suits and shoes? We called out to some of the looters to bring the jewels across the street so that we could buy them. Being street-wise, we knew the early morning junkies were having a field day looting for their fix. If we could lure them our way, we possibly could get some expensive jewels for little or nothing. But the brothers and sisters ran in the opposite direction as if they'd struck it rich.

Within a few hours, things were completely out of control. Now it's daylight and people awakened to join the looting from the pawnshops and stores on the block south of Joy Road. Police cars came and we left the scene, headed back to the west side of Detroit.

We were about three blocks from our destination when "The Big Four" pulled us over. I watched as one of them planted a .25 automatic pistol on the front seat of my friend's new convertible.

"Who does this gun belong to?" one of them asked after placing it there.

"The Big Four" in those days were the terror cops of Detroit. They consisted of three cops in plain clothes and one in uniform. The one in uniform shook nervously pointing the shotgun to our heads. Westside began to curse him, calling him every nasty name he could think of. I looked toward the sky knowing we were dead men. But the Lord had mercy on us poor fools. A voice came over their radio: "Emergency...there is a riot on Twelfth Street." One of the plain clothes men told the others, "F—k these niggers; we have a bigger job to do." We sat there looking at each other, relieved, not understanding the mercy of the Lord. I can look back now and see the hand of the Lord in my life to save me for such a time as this.

We relaxed at Westside's place for a couple of days, because the National Guard controlled the streets. Our rest was short lived, however, when a call came from the dope house informing us that jewelry and other valuables were being traded for drugs. We were aware of the nature of people who sold jewels for drugs. We could make a killing if only we could get through the streets flooded with National Guards. Greed said take the chance. The side streets and alleys became our route to the dope house on Twelfth Street and Pingree. We made a stop at a friend's house for safety precautions at the halfway point. It wasn't safe there. The National Guard shot up the side of his house when we peeped out of the window. They drove tanks through our communities shouting through a bullhorn demanding we lie on the floor and remain there.

> "We were about three blocks from our destination when 'The Big Four' pulled us over."

Finally we pressed our way to the dope house. The brothers and sisters had burned down the city and looted everything. The stolen goods were in circulation, and they were plentiful. The white store merchants invited the brothers and sisters to come in and take all they wanted, but "Please," they said. "Don't burn down our business." The community was fed up with racism, and most white faces were seen as the enemy. The brothers and sisters took all they could, then burned the stores to the ground. It was senseless and sad, but it happened. We're still paying the price.

The riots had been very good to a young lady who had sold all kinds of merchandise in the dope house. As we walked into the dope house she was on her way out. I apparently caught her eye, because after greeting each other she immediately flashed some diamonds before my eyes.

She "chose" me on the spot, giving me jewels and cases of expensive whiskey. I took her to her room at the Rio Grand Motel on West Grand Boulevard where she had much more merchandise. She gave it all to me and went back out to work. In the pimp game, it is mandatory for a prostitute or thief when choosing a man that she *"break herself."* That is, to give up everything, so that she can go out and bring in more, including another woman to help her.

She was a professional thief, who weighed about a hundred pounds, and could steal sweet out of sugar. The girl stole for me faithfully for months. She was in and out of the most expensive stores every day bringing home goods to fence (sell to another in bulk), but what I liked I kept.

In retrospect, I thought all of these women loved me and I believe some of them cared in their own way. We were all caught up in a way of life, or should I say the way of death! All of us were deceived by Satan and on our way to hell. It truly frightens me when I think of the faces of people in my past life and how they may be burning in hell forever. I love our Lord because of His mercy. His desire is that none should perish. I personally thank God that I was not easily consumed, because the mercies of God did not fail me. He kept me for a purpose.

Looking back over my life I can see God molding me for His glory. He has always allowed me to enter into situations that caused pain. The only pleasure in pain is that you come out with power. However, He has always allowed me to triumph over the situation. Even when I was in sin, God kept His hand of mercy around me to bring me to these days. Listen, I've been there. I know the way out. For how can we help others out if we've never been in?

Born A Bastard, Now Born Again

The Feds Are Coming!

The FBI was closing in on me because I had not responded to the military draft. I was so out of touch with the real world that I was not aware of the war in Vietnam. The street life had beat me down. I visited my Aunt Vera, and she greeted me with a letter "inviting" me to enter into the U.S. military or pay a five-thousand dollar fine and go to Leavenworth prison.

I failed the test for the U.S. Army, but passed the most difficult test to enter into the U.S. Navy. I was glad to enter into the Navy. I remembered my Uncle Arthur Calvert and how handsome he looked in his uniform when coming home on leave. If I'd gone into the Army, I believe there was a body bag waiting for me. Infantry was more dangerous than sailing. God had a plan for my life that's unfolding to this day, and I thank him I'm still alive.

I was pleased with the option. I would not go to jail or pay a fine. I packed my bags and left for basic training at NTC San Diego where I began to learn principles and find my position in life. I had led women the wrong way all of my life; now I would lead men the right way. I was impeccable in appearance and with my personal belongings. Other companies were brought to my area to view it as a model on how to keep the military standard.

God gave me favor with an officer by the name of Chief Burke. Early one morning, as we fell in line for inspection before marching to chow, he handed me the sable (a type of sword), giving me charge of the whole company. We won every flag that could be won in basic training, achieving the highest honor in boot camp.

I could not believe a white man in the position Chief Burke held could love me. This was the first time a white man had demonstrated genuine love. He even invited me into his lovely home in the hills of San Diego and allowed me to swim in his pool. Basic training was a turning point for me and were some of the best days of my life.

On graduation day from boot camp, Company 363 marched in front of the military brass, their families, and our families. It was called "passing in review," where all companies marched and were known by the flags they carried. Company 363 had all of the flags as we passed by the military brass, and I was their leader. Down through the years, God has been good to me.

While in boot camp, I met a young man from Los Angeles. He told me about his neighbor and what a wonderful person she was. I met her and we became friends. I had no idea she would soon become my first and only wife.

The Orient

Allow me to take you to the Orient where Satan planted more seeds of deception. I have learned that the person who knows Jesus Christ benefits from the increase God gives. For those who do not know him, the devil can cause increase as well, but it is always towards their destruction, not their deliverance. The Spirit of God in a person helps to plant for a good harvest. The spirit of the devil will plant for increase, but it is a bad harvest.

The bad seed that had been planted in me, and had been watered through disobedience, was renewed. Prostitution, drinking, and drugs were prevalent even in a world as different as the Orient. The same devil, just a different environment. I believe Satan's assignment in the Orient and Third World countries is ten times worse than in the U.S. After traveling around the world, I can truly say that God has blessed America.

Before landing in the Philippines, we were informed of Subic Bay, Alongapo City. We were warned of little children who begged for pesos, and as soon as you turned your back they snatched your wristwatch. Sailors who had toured the Orient in times past told us exciting stories of easy sexual encounters with many ladies. Needless to say, after weeks and weeks of boot camp we were ready.

I don't have words to describe Alongapo City, except the town was small with dirt roads and a sewer smell. The taxicabs were everywhere, coupled with army jeeps painted in psychedelic colors ready to take you to the live part of town called the jungle where all of the "brothers" hung out. As you may know, black men may have been under-represented in the professional ranks, but we were over represented in the Vietnam War.

Our hearts burned when our ears picked up the melody of the "Motown Sound" coming from the clubs. We could swear that The Temptations, Smokey or some of the other Motown groups were there. As we entered the clubs, we were shocked to see Philippine young men on stage who played, sang, and sounded exactly like the groups we loved so much back in the states. To top things off, all of the clubs were filled with young, pretty girls waiting to entertain us. The sound of the music attracted us, and the girls were waiting to trap us. We were attracted to be distracted. At the entrance of Alongapo City we exchanged our money for their pesos. The rate was eighty of their dollars for twenty of ours. It was party time for us!

> "Our hearts burned when our ears picked up the melody of the Motown Sound . . ."

The first very gorgeous woman who approached me became my lover and friend. A prostitute purchased weed for me and protected me from the thugs. She slept with me until it was time to go back on base aboard ship. She never complained about anything, and whatever I gave her monetarily was okay. You could not tell me then that having a prostitute and living the nightlife was not the good life.

This young girl must love me, I thought. No matter how drunk I was that night, she never stole from me and always made sure I was headed back to the base on time. She would oftentimes promise me that if I ever did "butterfly" (see another woman), she would cut my throat. You could not tell me this wasn't love. I encountered the same experiences in China, Japan and even Australia, an incredible place.

The Old Testament speaks of the days of Joshua. Joshua was the man chosen by God to lead the Israelites once they crossed over the Jordan River into the Promised Land. Joshua was Moses's replacement. He sent two of his soldiers to spy out the land. The Bible says, they went and came into a harlot's house named Rahab, and they lodged there. Now, the real purpose for the soldiers lodging at Rahab's house was to bring salvation for the glory of God. There is also a purpose for all of my lodging and encounters with prostitutes, and that's to write this book to inform you that the wages of sin is death. To preach the salvation of the Lord, which promises eternal life.

Please pray this prayer now!

Father of Heaven, I am unclean in your sight. I thank you for having mercy upon me and sparing my wretched life such as it is. I know you must love me to allow me to remain in your sight as filthy as I am. Just as you saved Rahab in the days of old, please save me now. You are the same God yesterday, today, and forever. Please wash me in your Blood and make me clean. Come into my heart right now with your precious sweet Holy Spirit and give me rest. In Jesus' wonderful holy name I pray. Amen.

Don't you feel better? Now find some water and get baptized in Jesus' name. My friend, this is just a start, a beginning of a new life for you. The Bible says that we are all dead in our sins. We all fall short of what God has for us. But Jesus is our way out. Let me continue.

A Sovereign God

When I was overseas, the devil watered the seed he had planted in me on Twelfth Street. I have learned that nothing can pass our way unless it crosses the desk of God. When the devil tries to rule our lives, God overrules! Unbeknownst to me, while I was experiencing a life of sin on the beach, God was blessing me aboard ship while off the coast of Vietnam. He blessed me to be a radioman, which was a field not open to many blacks at that time. I had a radio show aboard the ship, U.S.S. Camden

84

(AOE-2) while in Vietnam, entertaining the troops after work hours. This made me popular among the troops. God in His sovereign will for my life was letting me know there was more to me than whores and partying. He knew I had always wanted to be a broadcaster, and He allowed it to happen. He was drawing me unto Himself all the time.

Deeper Depths

To further compound my twisted mind that sex with whores, parties, and drugs were the true way of life, for the first time in my life, I snorted pure heroin and smoked the most potent marijuana in the world. Deceived, I felt I needed substances instead of the "substance of things hoped for and the evidence of things not seen" (*see Hebrews 11*). I just knew that drugs were all I needed to make it big in life. That deception later almost cost me my life and eternity in hell.

Restless Soul

I came back to the United States in 1972 with an *Honorable Discharge* after serving four years in the U.S. Navy. I began to pursue a career in radio while attending junior college. I landed a job selling insurance and married my first and only wife, Patricia Stewart. I met her before boarding the Navy ship. My wife attended Pepperdine University and worked as a telephone operator. She was also a good Christian girl.

The Scriptures explain, *"Therefore shall a man leave his father and mother and shall cleave unto his wife and they shall be one flesh" (Gen. 2:24).* We were very happy in those days. We even made the "Newlywed Game" show on television. Our marriage was blessed until I turned it into a curse.

I began to get restless with the little pay I was receiving selling insurance, and my radio career seemed to be on hold. So I began to visit one of my old Navy buddies with whom I got high on the ship while sailing the Gulf of Tonkin in Vietnam. My white buddy and I would serve on the same watch in the radio

> "But how many of you know that the devil can use the people closest to you to bring you down?"

shack aboard ship, and would go back to the transmitter room and smoke the "best" hashish in the world. I left Canoga Park, California, that day with a few pounds of marijuana to sell. No one could tell me at that time that he was not my friend. But how many of you know that the devil can use the people closest to you to bring you down? I believe to this day he liked me as a friend, but we were both spiritually dead.

Isn't it interesting that people of the world sometimes help each other more than children of light? *Luke 16:8* reminds us that our Lord praised the *"unjust steward"* because he had done wisely.

"The children of this world," Jesus said, *"are in their generation wiser than the children of light."* When the rich master suggested firing the unjust steward, he immediately reduced the debts of those who owed him. He helped those who owed his boss, so when he would be fired he could get a favor from those he had helped. This is the way of the people of the world. Although they help each other in evil doing, they help. The intention is good, but the motive or reason is wrong. My white friend meant well to give me the weed to sell to make some extra money, but it was a trick of the devil.

Born A Bastard, Now Born Again

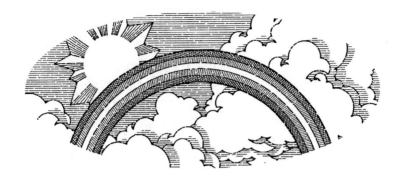

The Poison: Almost Made It To Hell!

I began to deal marijuana on a small time basis until I was introduced to a gentleman in 1973 who was a major player in the heroin game. I knew nothing about this game, but soon found out it was the fastest money and also the dirt of all dope games. When I saw him in his big house on the hill, swimming pool in the back yard, new Cadillac with a car phone, and fancy jewels, I was attracted and tempted to try this deadly and dangerous game. The catch was when he showed me a bundle of money from a recent sale. It's like when the people were introduced to the first Israelite king, Saul, in the book of *I Samuel*. They saw Saul's height and handsomeness. They forgot about God and wanted Saul for their king. And you know what was ironic? My friend's name was King. Like those ancient Hebrews, I was blinded by Satan and was on my way to eternal death. **The enemy gives good gifts.**

The Con Game

I left my job at the clothing store on the day they promoted me. This was one of the worst mistakes I've made in my life. Two twin brothers would come into the store where I worked, spending money like crazy. We became friends. They introduced me to the jewelry game. I left with them to go on the road with a con game selling fake jewels. We made much money, and I bought my first new 1974 Coupe Deville Cadillac. I thought for sure that God had smiled on me. *"There is a way that seemeth right to a man, but the end is the ways of death" (Proverbs 14:12).* I thought I was in order. After all, I was only tricking white people out of their money. I was sending my money home to my wife to save for us to get ahead in life. We had a right to have a new Cadillac. After all, white people had dogged us from slavery until now, and I did not force them to buy the jewels. In fact, they thought they were tricking me by paying so little for my "expensive" jewels that cost me pennies.

In my sinful way of thinking, this had to be a blessing from God, because I took money from people who had it to give. I did it with a sad story and sometimes with a smile. *Hosea 4:6* tells us that, *"My people are destroyed for the lack of knowledge." Proverbs 1:7* tells us that *"The fear of the Lord is the beginning of knowledge: but fools despise wisdom and instruction."* I did not know God. I despised wisdom and instruction from the manager at the store where I worked to make an honest living. Instead I fell for the fast life, which resulted in me almost los-

> **"Instead, I fell for the fast life, which resulted in me almost losing my life while in the depths of sin."**

ing my life while in the depths of sin. "What would it profit a man," Jesus said, "if he gain the whole world and lose his soul" (Matt.16: 26)?

Greed is Sin

We sold fake jewels for many months. We made a lot of money all over the country. Our game was solid. We would go to city hall in each state, pay for a peddler's license and then go to work tricking everyone in sight, including some greedy police.

Greed is one of the greatest enemies to mankind, and it rears its ugly head in the con game. For the con man, the money is never enough; the more he gets the more he wants. The one being "conned" is often equally guilty. He or she wants something for nothing, and will pay much to get nothing. Greed is a tool of the devil, but patience is of God. That's why the Lord said in Philippians 4:6-7 to, "Be careful for nothing, Don't be anxious for anything, but in every-thing by prayer and supplication let your requests made known unto God. And the peace of God, which passeth all understanding will keep your hearts and minds through Christ Jesus."

We are also instructed in the book of **Proverbs 3:5-6** to, *"Trust in the Lord with all your heart, and lean not to your own understanding, but in all thy ways acknowledge him and he will direct thy path."*

The Power Of Satan and Drugs vs. Jesus and the Power of the Spirit

So here I am, driving a new 1974 Caddie and selling fake jewels in and around Los Angeles, California. I was tired of being out of town all the time and away from my new wife. But I had a need to reach higher heights in the underworld. Working through the channel of greed, Satan made sure I became friends with one of the biggest heroin dealers of that time. I was introduced to a fast money-maker, and managed to involve myself in the deadliest game in the underworld. Through this experience I learned about the everyday junkie.

All junkies are not on the street corner begging for dope. Some are salesmen. Others are sleeping in the bed with you. We have people that use heroin from all walks of life, from the gutter to the highest levels of business and government. In my involvement with the dope game–both selling and using–I found out on a very personal level what the junkie is feeling and why they steal and will kill for the dope.

I was sitting in my apartment in Inglewood California, just "chilling." It amazed me how these few people I was serving were giving me all this money. What was it in this little package that they just had to have? Why would they beg for it when their money was short? Why would women offer sex for it? Now that I know Jesus, I'm aware of whose voice told me to open one of those packs to see how it felt to be high from heroin. God will never tell us to get high on dope, but the devil and our flesh will. So I did, and the feeling was so wonderful that I tried it for days and was almost hooked. It feels good, but it's death!

When a person uses heroin, the body develops a sick dependency. The user cannot function without it. Therefore the junkie is always sick until he or she gets a "fix." The fix will sustain them until the dope wears off. Then the body craves for more. The more you put into the body, the more it craves. Therefore you can begin using a twenty-five dollar pack, and within a little while you will need a one-hundred dollar pack. The person who cannot afford to pay one-hundred dollars a day has to steal or kill to get "well" just for a little while. Then the sickness begins again. It is a vicious cycle, and it is of the devil.

The junkie spends all of his life stealing. Most typically, the male junkies steal and the female junkies steal and sell their bodies. Both are searching for a void that is never filled, unless they give body and soul to Jesus.

To be bewitched is to have a spell cast over you. Anyone who will sell their child, sell their body to anyone who comes along, insensitive to death or to others is under a spell. That's what drugs will do to the addict.

Satan transforms himself into a puff of smoke in the crack pipe. He performs one of the greatest magic tricks of all times: entering into the soul of the person smoking and casting a spell on the mind of that weak vessel. The person believes that they have experienced the greatest high ever. It even magnifies sexual gratification. But you can never satisfy your flesh. It will take you to the dust with it. But your soul can live in Jesus Christ.

The drug user is bewitched by the dealer's dope. They look up to him as "The Great One." That's why the user gives up all of their dignity, money, jewels, deeds to their home, car and all they possess to the drug dealer, thinking he can give them the solution to their problems. And all the time he is giving them false power, empty thrills, and death.

The drug dealer has a special power over his sick customers. I'm so ashamed to admit that I received wealth at the expense of the sickness of others. Any person without the virtues of God is blind and cannot see afar off (**II Peter 1:9**). I could not see family ties broken because of the product I sold. I was blinded and drawn by the lure of money, and the false power I held over the user.

I have a special anguish in my heart for women who are tricked into this life. In the book of Genesis, we find that the woman is taken from the man in creation. She is drawn to him, as he is to her — to his side, the place where she was pulled from and fashioned into a woman by God Himself. Man is made to possess power. But here lies the devil. He will draw you to a man who only possesses false power. The woman clings to a drug boy because of the bundles of money, cars, clothes, and jewels. Woman came from man so she seeks her place beside or in most cases behind the power. She will do just about anything to retain her position. Some women will even try to adjust to the abuse or to the other woman just to be with the power. When the devil distracts her from God and attract her with the lure of drug money, he draws her to the false power of the dealer.

Even women in the church look to be with the "dope boy." The ugly, slang name for these women is "sack chaser." It is so unfortunate that many of our daughters are dead and dying or in prison or on their way because they seek the false power of the devil, by yoking themselves with the dope dealer. And sad, too, for the dealer who is himself being led by an illusion from the devil, because his end is death.

"Come out from among them, and be ye separate," says the Lord, for what fellowship has darkness with light, touch not the unclean thing; and I will receive you (II Corinthians 6:17).

The Real Power

After more than twenty years in "the game," I was finally caught. I sat in Federal prison for five years and eight months. I could not think of one person who made it out of the dope game – including myself – without tragedy. Either something tragic happened to their family or they went to jail for many years and lost everything, or they were killed very tragically themselves.

We perish because we lack knowledge. Here then is wisdom: Come to Jesus, all of you who are seeking false power. He will give you rest. Yoke up with him. His yoke is easy and his burden is light. He is the real power. Anyone who rose from the dead has the real power, *all* power. Accept Him today and allow Him to rise up in you and give you the real power you need. Anyone who can say, "I am He that liveth and was dead; and behold I am alive for evermore, Amen. And I hold the keys of hell and death"— that Person is the right One to know. I hope you feel the same. Accept Him and live; reject Him and die.

Power of Drugs

I have a heavy burden at this time to further expound on the subject of drugs. If you will allow me, let us look a little deeper into the life of Simon the drug dealer in the book of Acts. We're looking at Acts 8-9. Here is the passage. **A man named Simon had been a sorcerer...for many years, claiming to be someone great.**

The Samaritan people, from the least to the greatest, often spoke of him as "The Great One — the great power of God." He was very influential because of the magic he performed. It is recorded that they all gave heed (they respected him as if he was doing a great work in the community, the big man in town). The people who purchased a small amount to the person that could afford any amount went by Simon's house for their fix.

When I was dealing drugs, the $25 a day junkie purchased from me. The entertainer that could afford to sit and smoke all day bought dope also. From the least to the greatest, they got their fix, the same as in Simon's day. The people in his day thought that he was the great power of God. Likewise, women and men worshipped me, because I had good drugs.

I found out later in life that it was a love — hate relationship between the user and the dealer. But because I was a "ladies man," I was able to misuse women at will. Any of them that looked up to me as some great guy paid in some way or the other. Many of the sex parties were attractive because of the drugs that were available. Grown men have begged for it and I have almost lost my life many times dealing it.

> "Women and men worshipped me, because I had good drugs."

Deadly Setup

A "crack head," a person addicted to the most deadly form of cocaine smoked through a pipe, called one day for a package and set me up. As I pulled into the motel parking lot near Hollywood Boulevard, where I was to meet him, by instinct I turned my Caddie around heading out of the parking lot. Two men pulled along beside me and pulled out badges pretending to be the police. They shot up my car, but they missed me. I pulled off in my Coupe Deville, driving frantically searching myself for blood. God had mercy on me in spite of myself, which is one of the many reasons I am so grateful to Him.

There was another time I trusted my cousin's girlfriend. Late one night, she called and ordered some rock cocaine. I agreed to let her come, but when I opened the door, a long gun was put in my face. The robbers took the dope and a little money, my semi-automatic machine gun, and told me to lie on the floor and put a pillow on over my head. I just knew they were going to shoot me in the head. But the hand of God was upon me, and I'm still here without a hole in my head. Glory to God! I share these experiences with you so that you can know that Satan will kill you. Please stop now, and call upon the name of the Lord to help and deliver you from this evil. His name is Jesus!

When Simon the sorcerer saw the miracles and signs, which were done by the apostles of Jesus Christ, especially when he saw them lay hands on people and they received the Holy Ghost, he offered them money. He tried to pay for the power of God. I thought I was a friend of God because I would occasionally drop a $50 bill into the church offering once a year. You could not tell me that God and I were not the best of buddies after I made a U-turn in the middle of the street in broad daylight to give a $10 bill to a bum who sat on the bus bench sleeping. After all, taking my time to turn my new Cadillac around to help a bum with money made selling dope and pimping women was the greatest thing I could do for God. But my brothers and sisters, we cannot pay God off for our sins. You won't be able to buy your way out of hell. To find favor with God, just accept his son Jesus Christ as your Lord and Savior. The Bible tells us in **Romans 5:1, "Therefore being justified by faith we have peace with God through our Lord Jesus Christ."** To be justified is to be pardoned from everything you've done wrong.

To believe on the cross of Jesus Christ is to be justified, just as if you have been clean and free all of your life from sin and death. To receive this new life, your fine car can't ride it in, your luxury house can't live it in, your fine jewels can't shine it in, all the sex in the world can't satisfy it in, but you must be born-again (by the water and Spirit).

My friends, There is nothing new under the sun. I'm more than sure that in more ways than one, Simon accommodated all of those virgins back in the Bible days who wanted a temporary high. For the women who were already sexually active, it was no big thing for them, and "par for the course" for Simon.

But Simon wanted to be like the disciples, to lay hands on people and convey the gift of the Holy Ghost. In **Acts 8:20**, Peter answers him: **"Thy money perish with thee, because thou hast thought that the gift of God may be purchased with money."** My brothers and sisters, God doesn't need our money.

"The earth is the Lord's and the fullness thereof, the world and all they that live in it belong to Him" (**Psalm 24:1**). The Bible also says in **Psalm 22:29,** *"All they that be fat upon earth (the rich dope dealers, gangsters, call girls, casino owners, night club owners) shall eat and worship: all they that go down to the dust of the earth shall bow before him."* We must all go by way of the dust of the earth.

No matter how good we look, or how much money we have, all of us will die someday. No one can keep his own soul alive. Jesus is the Savior of the soul and only the Savior can keep us from falling and present us faultless and blameless before the presence of his glory with exceeding joy.

Please at this time and at this very moment, if you are in sin and fit the nature and character of Simon the dope dealer, pray this prayer now!

Dear God, I need a heavenly Father in my life today and forever. Please have mercy on me according to your loving kindness, and please blot out everything I've done wrong. Wash me in the blood of Jesus and make me clean. Now Lord, create in me a clean heart Oh God! And renew within me a right spirit. I believe that Jesus Christ died for my sins and I accept him as my Lord and Saviour. I believe that He was buried and rose from the dead according to the Scriptures for my justification. I now desire to be baptized in His precious name. Amen.

Oh God, Don't Let Me Die in This Place

In Early October 1974, late in the evening, I received a call from Lucifer through a young man I'd known in the past. It was a call of desperation, a growling voice! I now understand that he was under the influence of an evil spirit. This guy knew that I was a dealer, but I did not realize he was sick and needed a fix. I had not associated with him for months. Not listening to my first mind, I went to see what his cry was all about. "I have a great deal for you," he said. When I went to see him, I immediately knew it was a set up. When I did not submit to the robbery and turned my back to leave the scene, I heard a noise. When I tried to move faster my whole body gave way to the ground. I collapsed and tried to crawl to my new Cadillac while he searched my pockets for dope and money. I remember looking at a bright light in the sky and begging God not to let me die like this.

I found out that very night it is most important where we die and whose we are when we die. I was told later that I almost died in the hospital. I lost my leg, but not my soul. But I am not bitter. *"For it is profitable for thee that one of thy members should perish and not that thy whole body should be cast into hell (Matthew 5:29)."* Praise the Lord!

This poor man cried and the Lord heard him and saved him out of all his troubles (*Ps. 34:6*). In that fateful month, my soul would have entered into hell forever. But God, Who is rich in mercy, for his great love wherewith he loved me even when I was dead in sin, had already sent Jesus to the cross to die for my sins. I thank God I lost a leg and not my soul. I know for sure that when God has a purpose for your life, no demon from hell can prevent that purpose. Man is utterly powerless before the purposes of God! In fact, you cannot even kill your own self.

Big Al Is Born

With the goodness of God, rehabilitation, and the love of my wife Patricia, my confidence grew and I enrolled in the Los Angeles School of Broadcasting. I excelled there and graduated the top student in my class. In fact, I was on the air in a major market station even before I graduated. This was the fulfillment of a childhood dream.

I had always desired to be a professional broadcaster. When I was in the Navy aboard ship, I was given a radio show that the troops greatly appreciated. After my discharge, I worked in Thousand Oaks and also Bakersfield California as a radio DJ. But now I'm on the air in a major market on a major station. I found my gift and public appreciation in broadcasting.

I excelled in radio and was having a great time until I went to work one morning and found the door was padlocked by the I.R.S. This was one of the biggest letdowns of my life. Radio broadcasting had become the other "leg" I had lost.

Instead of pressing on to another station I decided that if the "legitimate" life had let me down, I knew how to help myself. I knew something else to do. I knew how to deal drugs. I had just lost a leg listening to the cry of the devil, but was willing to listen again to his call back into the streets in the dope game. I still had a bad spirit. That's why it's important to get saved and be born of the Spirit of God and be baptized in Jesus' name to have a change of heart and mind.

"If any man be in Christ, he is a new creature. Old things have passed away and behold all things are become brand new" (II Corinthians 5:17). In other words, once you are saved, your appetite will change. You won't want to do the same things you used to do and you won't want to go to the same places you used to go. Whatever God does to the human heart and mind for just believing on the cross of Jesus Christ is still a mystery, but it is right and it is very good. When we are not close to God, we think our way is right and good for us. But I'm a living witness that the Creator of all things knows what's best for everything and everyone.

By 1975, cocaine had become the primary drug among the night people, the dope men, pimps and whores, especially for recreational purposes (sex parties). I do not claim to know God's real purpose for creating cocaine. I do believe that the original purpose was real good. For me, it served as an aphrodisiac. I had begun "chipping," or using it sporadically, just before the radio station closed. I knew the heroin game, but being dead in trespasses and sin I picked up the coke sack again. Satan introduced me to some of his biggest demons and its dangers. After

> "I know now that the Lord was working on me all the while I was in sin."

all, it had almost cost me my life. I know now that the Lord was working on me all the while I was in sin.

My cousin sold angel dust or PCP. When I watched him cook it with ten to twelve dangerous chemicals, one of them called, *"Red Devil Lye,"* it bothered me to think that we would be selling it to another human. Just to think of people consuming such a horrible drug touched my conscience in a way it had not been touched before. That's how I know now the Lord was already working on me. The cookout was so dangerous that men have been blown up or burned severely. But *for the love of money is the root of all evil,* and we did it for the money. I was invited to the "cookout" as they called it, because my cousin wanted to introduce me to the PCP game. He knew I was a good dope salesman, and I would help make him more successful. I witnessed chemical interactions that looked like they would kill a gorilla on the spot. I took it and sold it, and people bought it as if it were gold. This body is fearfully and wonderfully made, to withstand such assaults and still heal itself.

And so now here I am back in the dope game with three sacks: *"the boy"* (heroin), *"the girl"* (cocaine), and *"the monster"* (PCP or Angel Dust). To top it all off, I had a ladies clothing store and a good looking booster (thief) stealing the finest of clothes to stock my store. All she wanted was a fifty dollar pack of heroin a day and sex.

Los Angeles has one of the largest garment districts in the world where I shopped daily for the ladies. So here I am, driving a new Cadillac, with three different kinds of drugs to sell, a ladies clothing store, dressed to kill everyday, women wanting to be with me, willing to work on all of the whore strolls, bringing me their money. I had fun with women who loved to undress outside of the dressing room trying on clothes in my store, in sunny southern Los Angeles, California. But little did I know, this was all a trick of Lucifer to take my soul to hell forever.

My sales girl, who was a beautiful, light-skinned Jamaican woman, fell in love with me and in her off time went and sold her body to bring me money. Satan had entangled and trapped me with everything he thought I liked. To further compound my trip to hell, the most beautiful young woman came into my store on a rainy day. She was very pretty and brown with long black hair. I had to have her and did. I made her my number one lady. She would go to the street and make money before I got out of bed. I fell in love with her, but mistreated her because she was a whore.

By now my wife had divorced me after our first

and only child. I had lost all sense of family values. I tried to reconcile my marriage, because I loved my wife and my daughter, but I was a dead man walking in trespasses and sin, using cocaine, snorting heroin, and having sex with numerous woman. I was caught up between the street life and family. And like a fool, I chose the streets. There is nothing worse than the spirit of the devil in a man.

Brothers, drop the dope sack and pick up your family and love them just as faithfully as you sold that dope. When the real deal goes down all you have is God first and your family. The devil comes to destroy you and your family!

"The devil, the thief, came not but for to steal, to kill, and to destroy" (John 10:10). Crack is the mother of many demons that come to steal, to kill, and to destroy you.

Crack Up, Life Down

I was at the home of my "cocaine connect" in one of the most affluent neighborhoods in Los Angeles purchasing my sack for the weekend business. He led me to a bedroom where there was a whole platter full of drugs on the bed, and told me he would be with me in a moment. I never was a petty thief, so I just sat there and stared at the dope wondering when he would come and fix my sack so that I could be on my way. The waiting lasted for about an hour or more, which seemed a lifetime. He finally came and brought me to the room where he and this very attractive lady were sitting. He introduced her as an airline hostess who flew from Los Angeles to San Francisco. She was teaching him how to freebase.

He began to show me what she had showed him. It was a process of crystallizing the cocaine, preparing it to smoke in a pipe. Now that I am saved and filled with the precious Holy Spirit, I can see that Lucifer transformed himself into a puff of smoke and attempted to control me. I can see where he brought many demons from hell and placed them in the lives of major players in the dope and pimp game, both men and women in all of our major cities. I literally watched the destruction in the lives of many money-making people who lived in houses on the hill, drove the Rolls Royce, and the Benz. This is an account of how the drugs moved in among men who were gentlemen but lived in the underworld. This is also an account of how Satan destroyed the lives of some of the biggest dope men in the  country and spread his demons throughout their families in the form of freebase, which is now known as crack, and destroyed them all. He turned the riches he had given them into rags.

Eventually the quality of cocaine I purchased became worse and worse. My supplier was smoking up his profit and skimming from my pack. Just a few years later, I found out he lost his home and died in a motel on a whore stroll while smoking crack.

I was introduced to another dope man, Georgie Porgy, and we became the best of friends. We had everything we wanted: new Cadillacs, jewels, women, and drugs. Beautiful ladies would go with me to Porgy's house just to smoke the pipe and serve me sexually because of the dope. Dope is a terrible thing!

Porgy had a beautiful home on the outskirts of L.A. and I could go there to smoke and party. The "square people" (lay people) had not even heard of freebase, because it was processed and smoked in private among a select group of players who had money and dope. Most of the drug society knew about snorting, but nothing about smoking. This is how it happened: We had the dope sack and money and began smoking recreationally and unknowingly got hooked. It started out being fun, just partying in private. We began to take it to the after hour clubs where we would separate ourselves from the rest of the crowd in a room and smoke. I knew something was different when we would not share the dope when smoking as we did when snorting.

> **"We began to take it to the after hour clubs where we would separate ourselves from the rest of the crowd in a room and smoke."**

Curious onlookers (ladies) who we sensed were about big fun could smoke with us. Anytime a couple of men are together, wearing pretty jewels, pretty clothes, and having what seems to be fun, temptation is strong. In the game, men onlookers were insulted if they asked for another player's dope. No man cares to be told he needs lace around his underwear to smoke. But a pretty woman who wanted to have fun could smoke for a while. Many of them were hooked also and would perform any kind of sex act just to smoke.

Over a period of a few months, the "free base" changed the lives of most of the major players and pimps. Everyone who smoked the pipe had to sell more heroin to keep up the cocaine parties, because the profits received from the coke were smoked up.

I would frequent West Side Loan, my favorite pawnshop, to purchase some gold or diamonds. I had not allowed myself to get way out on the stuff. I basically kept it recreational, taking a puff with a freaky girl and her girlfriend. I could still afford some luxuries. While shopping at West Side Loan, I saw that some familiar jewels were up for sale. Players and their ladies had pawned their jewels and could not redeem them within the six-month period.

Most of us in those days wore unique jewels; some had their street name spelled out on their bracelet, so you knew Big Al's jewels when you saw them. These major players went from powerful to pitiful, from pawning their jewels and losing big houses and luxury cars, to begging for dope instead of selling it, from riding in luxury to walking and living in motels, all because of the all-consuming crack pipe. They lost their snobbish attitudes toward the lesser players, and made sorry attempts at friendships to anyone who held the Crack Sack. They began to rob others, sending crack-head women who would call late at night pretending for drugs or sex. They brought thieves with them, so that when the door was opened, you were met with guns and demands for drugs and money. Some of the major players were set up by their own workers who had turned into crack-heads and were let into their homes by wives and children who were used to seeing them as friends of the man of the house. But once inside, they demanded drugs and valuables. When resisted, they took their lives and the lives of their families.

It was a vicious cycle. Then, the problem hit the "square" people: church members, husbands and wives with nine-to-five jobs. None of these people could afford to smoke. If the habit had depleted the pockets of the big dope men and women who made great amounts of easy money daily, what do you think it did to the rest of society? Cocaine moved from the big nuts like wildfire throughout the mainstream of society–among doctors, dentists, lawyers, entertainers, politicians, and preachers. You name them–they were smoking the pipe.

My experience when smoking was that sexual pleasure was magnified and seemed more pleasurable with women who enjoyed the same. The high eclipsed everything, made everything seem better and more exciting. However, it was never enough. The flesh is never satisfied.

This is how Satan lure's people into his kingdom of hell. I truly believe this is the biggest hook that Satan has ever landed on planet Earth. It is one of the greatest evils known to mankind. These were demons taking many souls to hell.

God will deliver you right now if you just call on His name instead of chasing a ghost that will never be found. If you *"seek the Lord while he may be found, call upon Him while he is near,"* if you give up your ways and your thoughts, if you return to the Lord, He will pardon you and bless you in ways you can never imagine in your wildest dreams. He will surprise you with a joy and peace that will make you wonder what you ever saw in that pipe or in that life.

Gone For Broke

Now the dope sellers, large and small, are broke and in the streets petty hustling. All it takes is a coke habit and a couple of bad deals and you find yourself in the rear of the street life. But if your reputation was good, you could always get a small sack from someone to get back on your feet. Or maybe you were allowed to sit around the crack table and get a hit for "old times sake," based on past reputation and how well you were liked.

By this time, I had been introduced to the underworld method of "cooking" the coke with water and baking soda, forming it into a rock and bringing it to its purest form to sell to the smokers. This method was quickest yet. A simple household product called Arm & Hammer Baking Soda and some water could put you in business. The destroyer of all things good had simply made it quicker and easier for all of us to kill ourselves. He truly came to kill, to steal, and to destroy, but Jesus came that we have life, even the abundant life that we thought we were getting from serving the devil.

The Origins of "Crack"

Now the rock form was on the scene and everyone was smoking like crazy. It is faster and much more potent, and so a little went a long way. Then someone very greedy invented a substance called "blow up" to make the rock bigger so that we could get more for the money.

This is how the name "crack" came about. We would sit around shaving from the solid rock to put the shavings on the pipe to smoke. One of the former players who was broke and was there at the mercy of the smokers and who still had a dope sack said, "Man give me that little crack that's on the plate." He was too proud to be rejected for asking for the big rock so he asked for the little shavings from the rock. And thus the name crack was born and raised to the level that it is today.

Those who knew the heroin game had an edge over those who knew only the coke game. If the heroin dealer smoked crack, he had a backup sack of heroin to make up for what he smoked in cocaine. He might last longer, but eventually anyone who smoked the pipe would get broke. We kept our cars and jewels, acquiring even more jewels when smokers stole and pawned things to us with the intention of never coming back. I was partying with the dope girls, the square girls and the whores, on my way to hell dead in sin.

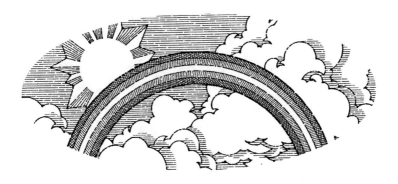

Fame and Shame in Hollywood

I had acquired a small fortune in jewels. My hands and wrist and neck were all lit up like a Christmas tree. I was wearing some of the most beautiful jewels in town, driving one of the prettiest Cadillac's in the city, and I had some pretty whores on the street corner's of L.A.; I now have a drug sack and am living in a condo overlooking the city.

People I had admired now looked up to me as if I was some great one. Owners of nightclubs catered to me. Famous entertainers visited my condo in the hills just to get away and to get high. Lucifer had me locked so deep into sin, I didn't even know that I was a sinner. My philosophy was, *"In this life, everyone has a chance to get rich, and this was just my time given to me by the Almighty."*

People were pawning their jewels to me. Young pretty girls were bringing me their best girl friends to party with so that they could get high. But this was all a trap of the devil to lure me, to rock me to sleep in sin until I met him in hell.

My Jamaican lady, who was light-skinned with short, black wavy hair and the prettiest legs in all L.A., decided to work on Sunset Boulevard in Hollywood, California. It became necessary to leave the Baldwin Hills area to ride the streets of Hollywood to "check my trap" to pick up the money.

One sunny day I was riding down Sunset Boulevard when the Hollywood police got behind me, and rode down on me to stop me. I swallowed a hand full of pure cocaine to keep from going to jail, enough dope to kill an elephant. When I felt my heart start to race out of my body, I went to my apartment and took a hand full of Valium to calm my heart down, and I didn't die. Bless the Lord, Oh My soul! When God has a plan for your life, you simply can't kill yourself. Bless the Lord with all that is within me.

My other ladies worked on the strips leading to the airport, which is the opposite end of the city from Hollywood. I kept very busy day and night from one end of the city to the other checking on my money. I became fascinated with Hollywood and the nightlife, especially when I saw Jack Nicholson in one of the clubs. But most of all, there were movie star-looking ladies on many of the streets and corners selling sex.

The Poison Continues

Then it came to me. I could set up shop right here in Hollywood. I found a motel and set up shop with the rock cocaine. I had beautiful jewels and was driving a new Fleetwood Cadillac, and had already become popular with some of the whores and pimps that were established in the area. Human nature is sometimes strange. When people see you in a winning position, they want to be with you. In or out of church, everyone loves to be around a winner.

My plan was to capture the Hollywood market. I would catch all of the loose whores (prostitutes without a man) who liked dope and get the whore money from the pimps who loved to smoke the pipe. I was like a kid in a candy store.

I eventually rented two apartments, in a building where many of the pimps and their whores lived, one to live in and the other to slang out of (sell dope). The rock cocaine business became so lucrative, sex with new women became so frequent that I began to neglect my ladies, and they soon ran off. I had already begun to experiment with a drug called "Citra Forte," a morphine-based cough syrup that provided a high for two days. I would actually nod in a state of ecstasy all day long. I began to use it to keep from having sex with the women who worked for me, so they could work longer hours. To counter the syrup high, I began to smoke the coke and take Valium to sleep. So here I am on one leg answering the door with a 38 revolver or sawed off shotgun, selling drugs while high on drugs.

I thank God for His mercy on me at a very stupid phase in my life. He protected me when I was doing everything possible to leave this earth while deep in sin. He protected me from robbers, murderers, jealous women, jealous men, and those, who out of greed or revenge, sought my life or my downfall. Most of all He kept me from myself. He is so wonderful to keep me alive so that I can warn you of the dangers of a sinful life. I must testify of His loving kindness toward me in Christ Jesus.

My sons and daughters, those of you just starting out in life, I have a word for you: "Enter not into the path of the wicked, and go not in the way of evil men. Avoid it, pass not by it, turn from it, and pass away" (Proverbs 4:14-15). You will save yourself a lifetime of sorrows and regrets.

I was set up for a robbery near Franklin Boulevard in Hollywood. The robbers shot up my car, but they missed me. I bought another new Fleetwood Cadillac, parked it at the car wash, got out to pay for the wash and someone jumped in and I guess they are still riding. To keep up my image, I began to rent stretch limousines. I moved out of Hollywood. I had caught a lady that was a dancer and began to play the nude clubs, selling coke to owners and dancers.

I bought a new, white Sedan Deville in 1985. Then was reacquainted with an old friend who gave me a pack of pure heroin. I began to make money and caught an oriental lady who loved to snort it. She took good care of me. We drove to Vegas and made some quick cash. For the first time in my life, I found myself hooked on drugs, in Las Vegas, sick as a dog. We came back to Los Angeles, and I made the mistake of bringing a black woman home to work with her. Niki got real angry and left. I never saw either of them again.

I moved back to Detroit with my son who was a baby at the time. I had made a contact in L.A. before leaving, and things began to click for me again. I began to make more money than I had ever made in my life. I began to get wealthy again. The devil was my father. He gave me fool's gold by the bags full, but his plan was to take me to hell.

Born A Bastard, Now Born Again

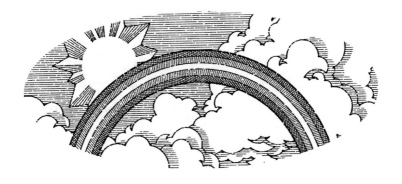

The Prison

I believe that God allowed everything in my past to happen. He set me up for a fall so that He could lift me up by His love. I began to make so much money I would literally get tired of counting it. I began to buy property and all the material things I so desired. In the process of purchasing some property I met a real estate broker and fell in love. We began to have great times together. I could afford to do anything she desired to do and more. I thought my life was complete, but God had another plan. I was king on the East and West coast, spending as I pleased. I made the championship fights during Ali's reign, taking pictures with celebrities, living the life (so I thought). After the partying, I began to notice a void was still in my life.

There was a police investigation going on in L.A. of which I was unaware. I had a phone conversation with a lady whose phone was tapped. The lady had sent me a large shipment, and one or two of the kilos had broken up during transit. The person on my end of town wanted the package to be solid for fear of tampering. I called and informed her that the library books she had sent me were not all she cracked them up to be. She copped the jive (understood the lingo).

But, unbeknownst to me, she was on a wire tapped phone telling her girl friend how much money I was sending to L.A and how fast I was sending it after she sent me a shipment. She also called my name to get her friend to remember who I was. This phone conversation, among other things, tied me into a conspiracy. I was arrested and extradited to L.A., and the judge required a one-million dollar bond

> "I knew I would go to jail when I read the affidavit that said, 'The United States of America vs. Alfred Lewis Calvert.'"

for my release (no ten percent; they wanted the full million). My first attorney, who was recommended by Neil Fink, met with me and ask for $250,000 before he could represent me.

The real-estate broker with whom I had fallen in love, and I love her to this day, raised the bond money when it was lowered to a half million dollars. I was one of the first individuals to be put on the tether, an electronic device that informs the Feds as to where you are at all times, in order to keep you from jumping bail. We fought the case for about two years and I went to prison for ten years. I knew I would go to jail when I read the affidavit that said, "The United States of America vs. Alfred Lewis Calvert." How could I beat the United States?

My ten years in prison began in Bastrop, Texas. Isn't it ironic that a bastard child is now doing time in prison in Bastrop, Texas? For the first time in a long time, I begin to feel like a failure. After a lifetime of telling others what to do, now here I am being told when to go to bed and when to get up, when to eat and what! My whole life was controlled by others in authority. I knew my two children would be taken care of, because I have that kind of family. But the thought of losing everything, especially the woman I'd just fallen in love with, caused much grief.

I believe that prison is the closest place to hell on earth than any other place. There are many things that you should know about my prison experience. I pray that the little I am sharing will keep you from going. Or, if you are already walking a walk of faith, that you will be moved to minister boldly behind the walls.

My military experience kicked in and I began to do my time in the same character and fashion as if I were on the street. I took pride in being clean and neat even in prison. Then one day after writing many poems about my past love life, suddenly, it occurred to me that, "I can do this." I was not going to fail, especially when I found out you could go to school. I enrolled in college and began to redeem the time.

When I began to turn my life around, the enemy got really angry and busy. He began to play with my mind concerning the beautiful woman I had fallen in love with and my children. I became depressed and downhearted. I began to write more poems about my love and our past lives together just to keep my sanity. I began to exercise and lose weight, conditioning my body in order to try and feel good about myself. But the loneliness and confusion only got worse. My plan was to get even with the system. I planned to get a good dope connection while in Federal Prison, and when I got out I was going to make them pay. "I'll sell dope and get rich all over again," I thought. Then I began to reflect on how I was raised in Shiloh Baptist Church. I found out about the church service in prison and began to attend.

I'm so thankful for this Word of God. If your children are raised in the church and go astray, rest assured that God will bring them back according to His Word. *"Train up a child in the way he should go: and when he is old, he will not depart from it."* *(Proverbs 22:6)*

The Power

I began to seek refuge in different ways: exercise, college, writing, and church. Then I began to hear the Word and to fellowship briefly with outside ministries that visited us from time to time. I began to read my Bible. Then I lost my sight, another enemy attack! I became oppressed and depressed again. The Feds chained me to a wheel chair and took me on the outside of the wall to an eye doctor. In retrospect, God gave me peace that day that I would be healed. Why would I lose my sight and I'm trying to learn about God? It was the beginning of a trying of my faith in Him, and a ministry that would soon heal thousands.

I continued to seek Him because I found some refuge in it. I found enough courage to call my Aunt Mildred who had done all she could to raise me properly after my mother passed when I was eleven years old. I must inform you that in prison there are two men to a cell, but somehow God had given me favor and placed me in an area where I had my own cell and shower. I was somewhat isolated, which allowed me to spend a lot of time in silence. My heart began to melt with sorrow for the wrong I had done.

I called my aunt and told her that I was in college and going to church in prison and I was sorry that I had disappointed her, and I apologized for the way things had turned out, assuring her that she had done very good in my up bringing. Her only reply was, "The Bible says to, *"Study to show thyself approved."* I did not understand what she meant but I knew if my Aunt Mildred told me something it was good for me and meaningful.

"Where can I find that in the Bible? I asked her.

"Find someone in the church," she replied.

"Ask him about a workman that need not be ashamed."

She put emphasis on the word *workman*! I hurried from the phone center, back to my unit to find this Scripture. I met a Jehovah Witness inmate who was on his way to his service, someone with whom I had already made friends. I asked him about the "workman" Scripture. He could not remember at the time, but promised me that before the day's end he would find it for me. I became thirsty and hungry for this Word that God had spoken through the only other woman besides my love that I knew I could trust. I became impatient and desperate for this Word of God. ***"Blessed are they, which do hunger and thirst after righteousness: for they shall be filled" (Matthew 5:6).***

That day, I had called my girl and she was very distant in conversation. In fact she had asked me not to call so much because of the phone bill. Prison is a strange environment. Things that happen behind prison walls, especially positive things, seem to magnify themselves as negative. I was downhearted, about out of my mind, I had been sightless, on one leg, and now it appears that I was womanless. I needed comfort just to keep my sanity. I couldn't wait for the Jehovah's Witness young man to show up. I needed something right now or I was going to lose it. So I began to search the Scriptures for myself.

Finally, my Jehovah's Witness friend showed up with the scripture about a workman in the Bible. Thanking him, I went back to my private cell, and once again I heard from the devil. "Look at yourself, in prison. Another man has Virginia; he has two legs and you've only got one, and you're in your forties. It is all over for you. You know she is with someone else every night." He tried to keep my mind on failure. He told me that I was hated, a bastard child in Bastrop Texas.

But I knew my aunt had given me something to comfort me. I finally found the Scripture: **II Timothy 2:15: "Study to show thyself approved unto God a workman that need not be ashamed, rightly dividing the word of truth."** This Scripture was good because Aunt Mildred gave it. However, the complete understanding was not clear, so it was not good enough to ease the pain. I continued to search the Bible for comfort and it seemed as if the devil had won. I could not understand much of what I was reading.

Then I came to a place in the Bible where it says, **"And ye have forgotten the exhortation which speaketh unto you as unto children, my son despise not thou the chastening of the Lord, nor faint when thou art rebuked of him" (Hebrews 12:5).** Just the words "my son" had an impact on me. This Scripture began to make sense to me. I began to reflect on my childhood and how I had forgotten how my aunt had raised me, and how I had gone my own way in life.

"There is a way, which seems right to a man, but the end of that way is death" (Proverbs 16:25).

I remember the brightest light shining through my window as I continued to read the Word. I understood not to blame God for my mistakes and to be strong as I bore the consequence of my mistakes. I then read the next verse, *"For whom the Lord loves he chastens, and scourges every son whom he receives" (Hebrews 12:6).*

Then it hit me. For years I felt that God hated me. After all, He had taken my mother at an early age, I had lost my leg, and now here I am in prison without the woman I knew He had given to me to love. I did not understand the chastening, but remembering old pirate movies I knew that scourging had something to do with whipping and punishment.

"How could God love me in the shape I'm in?" I thought.

I continued to read that *Hebrews* passage: *"If ye endure chastening God dealeth with you as with sons: for what son is he whom the father chasteneth not?"* I had never been a punk concerning enduring, so this part I was determined to deal with.

You must remember that all my life I carried the word "bastard" in my heart as a curse to me because of my out-of-wedlock birth. Nobody knew how this word hurt me but myself and God. I read *verse eight* in *chapter 12 of Hebrews* that says:

"But if ye be without chastisement, whereof all are partakers, then are ye BASTARDS and not sons." The words, "are ye" are key here.

The word that had hurt me all of my life came back to me, and before I could lose my mind from confusion or drop dead from a heart attack, that word *"bastard"* cut my heart, quick and powerful, sharper than any two-edged sword, piercing even the dividing of soul and spirit, joint, and marrow. That word discovered and revealed even the thoughts and intents of my heart.

I cannot begin to explain the magnitude of what happened that day. I began to weep uncontrollably, but I was not sad. Then I heard a voice very quiet and peaceful say to me, "You are not here because I hate you, but because I love you as my son. I wept for God knows how long. Joy came over me and I instantly knew that *I WOULD NEVER BE A BASTARD AGAIN BUT I WAS HIS SON.* **"This poor man cried, and the Lord heard him, and saved him out of all his troubles" (Psalm 34:6).**

My uncontrolled weeping was a cleansing. I began to understand the Word of God just a tinge more. As I continued to read the *ninth verse* I understood how I had feared and obeyed my daddy when he whipped me for disobeying him, and I loved him even more. It made sense to me to obey God and live! And just like my earthly daddy, I'd better learn to love God since I could not beat him back. My reasoning became clear. The eleventh verse made it clear as day that I was in a grievous situation: **"Now no chastening for the present seems to be joyous, but grievous: nevertheless afterward it yields the peaceable fruit of righteousness. . ."**

If I practice righteousness in my present situation, I understood that God would give me peace as He had done already, and peace was what I was looking for! I had to do right to live, and to live was my choice. In verse 12, He told me to straighten up and I did. I stopped weeping for a while and when I read verse 13 about the lame being turned out of the way, I knew I did not want that. I did not want to be apart from Him. Then he said, *"Let it rather be healed."* I knew I wanted to be healed and keep the same feeling of peace I witnessed at that time. He quickened me in my spirit (gave me life). Then in verse 14 He said, **"Follow peace with all men, and holiness, without which no man shall see the Lord."** I knew at that point I would seek the Lord at all costs, and I did.

"And you hath he quickened (GAVE LIFE) who were dead in trespasses and sin" (Ephesians 2:1).

In my weeping I called on the name of the Lord and He heard and answered me.

"Whosoever will call on the name of the Lord shall be saved" (Rom. 10:13).

After the weeping and calling on the name of the Lord, it seemed like a million pounds of pressure lifted off of me. Now that I'm saved, I know that it was love that lifted me.

I was sinking deep in sin, far from the peaceful shore, Very stained deep within, sinking to rise no more.

But the Master of the sea, heard my despairing cry, From the waters lifted me, now safe am I.

Love lifted me, love lifted me, When nothing else could help, love lifted me.

I was locked up under the law. But what the law could not do, God sent His Son Jesus to do.

Born A Bastard, Now Born Again

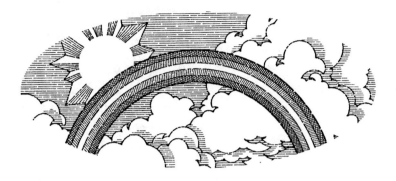

The Preacher

began to read the Word of God and meditate on it day and night. Fellowshipping with other people who were seeking God became important. Suddenly I realized that cursing had left my mouth. My days were brighter and my burden was lighter.

I met with my unit manager, who told me that I would spend all of my time in Texas. He sent the paperwork off to the region recommending that I go to Fort Worth, Texas because it was better equipped for the handicapped. However, the paperwork came back sending me to Milan, Michigan, where the Lord began to use me in a mighty way.

I was reading Isaiah, the sixth chapter, verses 1-8, and there received my calling. In *verse eight*, God asks the question, "Whom shall I send, and who will go for us?" I began to feel sorry for God that He had no one to help him. I began to weep out of control again, and I cried out with a loud voice, *"Send me–*

I will go." Then I read where Isaiah responded in the same manner. I've been going ever since.

One Saturday morning, as I sat in the chow hall I looked around the wall at all of the young men who were locked up. They all had faces of sorrow and death. There is one thing a man does not do in prison, and that is cry. I began to weep and no one saw me, because the Lord shielded me. I asked the Lord, why am I crying for these

> "God brought things in full circle to show me that we cannot trust in everthing we see or hear."

men? I'm in prison just as they are. The Spirit spoke to me and said, " You have something they don't have." God broke my heart that morning and gave me love and compassion for people.

I began to preach to anyone and everyone in the prison, not caring about the consequences. God gave me favor, and I had run of the whole prison. I could speak and men would begin to cry. Men would look for me to lead them to salvation. The church began to get crowded as well as the Bible studies. The visiting churches would call on me to preach, instead of using their own preachers. Hundreds and hundreds of prisoners were saved by the power of God. I would stand anywhere on the compound, and men would come to me and not know how they got there.

I walked around the entire line in the mess hall, led by the Spirit of God telling the good news to white, blacks, spanish, officers, the warden and many others everyday and never got caught, because the Lord gave me favor and shielded me. I laid hands on officers as they wept and confessed Christ through the power of God. An officer once in charge at Milan whom I encouraged in the Lord is now a deacon in a church today. I've preached there twice. The warden came to hear me preach and stayed the whole service. God gave me favor to work outside the prison gate in the prison office with civilians. My prison life consisted of fasting, praying, and meditating on God's Word day and night. The Spirit would wake me up at 3:00 a.m. and 4:00 a.m. and cause me to just meditate and remember the Word of God.

The same pimp that influenced me in the sixties was in prison with me in the nineties, and I led him to the Lord. We became the best of friends. In fact he was my prayer partner every day and my barber. He confessed to me that he was a fake in the sixties. When I saw him in the sixties, he drove an Eldorado, and always had three of four white girls with him. He would stand up in the after hours clubs and confess that he did not "eat black pepper." (His stable was all white. He only pimped white girls. The black girls did not have a chance to get with him). God brought things in full circle to show me that we cannot trust in everything we see or hear.

Even the Muslim community respected me. They invited me to be their keynote speaker during Black

History Month in February. They had invited one of their leaders from the outside to come in and speak also. He never got a chance to utter a word. I began to talk about Black history to get their attention. I moved to a black man carrying the cross of Christ. You know the rest. It was Jesus and him crucified until the meeting was over and the civilians had to leave the prison. God did great things for me in prison! I could write volumes on how God used me in prison.

The Lord released me from prison to a great ministry under the leadership of pastor William H. Murphy Sr., where I assisted him for three years bringing many souls to the kingdom, including the siblings of my biological dad Tom Johnson and most of their children and friends!

After my release from prison, I led my girl, the real estate broker whom I loved, to the Lord on Belle Isle in Detroit, Michigan. The Lord used me when I went to L.A. on vacation to minister to the man that taught me the hero-in game. I preached Jesus Christ and him crucified to all of his family. God assembled his family in his mother-in-law's home during the daytime through his sister-in-law who was my friend in my former life. He did not accept Christ that day, but he heard the Word of God.

The Lord used me to hold a Bible study in the home of Tom Johnson, my biological dad, where I led many souls to Christ including his children. As a result, his home is a day care and church run by my stepsister. The Lord used me to win William Herring to the Kingdom. Do you remember Bronco, my partner in the number's game? He came to hear me preach and joined the church that day. He remained true to the faith until the Lord took him home.

When he did not have an offering to give to the Lord he would put an I.O.U. into the offering basket and would make it good when he got his check. He told me that if I was preaching there must be a God somewhere, and he had found Him.

Then the Lord moved me to the greatest ministry in the country, Greater Grace, under the leadership of Bishop Charles H. Ellis III, where I teach Sunday School and work in various ministries, including prison. I've co-hosted a television show and my own radio program, and I have several articles in the Gospel Connection Newspaper. I travel according to the Lord's will and preach and teach in many churches in many cities. As I close, I've recently ministered from the pulpit of Bishop Noel Jones of Greater Bethany in Los Angeles, California. This was one of the greatest moments of my life.

I'm happy in the Lord and single with two beautiful adult children, daughter Kim and son Al, Jr.

This is my story: I was Born A Bastard; Now I'm Born-Again.

About the Author

My ministry in the Lord Jesus began while incarcerated. I was saved in prison called to preach and filled with His precious Spirit. Then the Lord began to use me to win countless souls for the kingdom in prison.

Although my degree is in business, my experience with people spans over forty years in the streets with pimps and prostitutes, drug dealers and people from all walks of life. More than that, I've been with and was taught by Jesus while incarcerated, fasting without bread or water for days in prayer and meditation in His holy Word.

My ability in pastoral leadership began while serving for three years as the assistant to Dr. William H. Murphy, Sr. of the *Greater Ebenezer Full Gospel Missionary Church.*

I have written this book, **"Born A Bastard, Now Born-Again."** It includes four phases of my life: (**1**) the pimp, (**2**) the poison, (**3**) the prison, and (**4**) the preacher. It details my experiences in seeking love in all the wrong places.

I've also poetically written on every book in the Bible titled, **"Divine Rhyme."** I have written several full-page articles in the *Gospel Connection Newspaper* on love and marriage, and also on law and grace.

I've worked both radio and television, hosting and co-hosting my own show. I teach Sunday school at *Greater Grace Temple, The City of David* under the leadership of Bishop Charles H. Ellis, III. I also work in various other ministries at Greater Grace, especially prison. I've ministered the Gospel of Jesus Christ all over the country, for which I am not ashamed.

I'm more than pleased to come to you for such a time as this. I owe everything to the Lord for his precious Blood, resurrection power, and the sweetness of His grace.

I'm blessed with two wonderful children: Alfred, Jr. and Kimberly Calvert.

God Bless,

Elder Alfred L. Calvert
Evangelist and Teacher

Born A Bastard, Now Born Again